Memoires of a Pauper Traveling with the King

Road to Royalty

Katherine Renteria

Memoires of a Pauper Traveling with the King
Copyright © 2021 Katherine Renteria
All rights reserved.
ISBN Print book: 979-8-458091824

Unless otherwise indicated, all scripture, quotations are taken from the King James Version of the Bible.

www.shekinahglorypublishing.org

(936) 314-7458

Shekinah Glory
PUBLISHING

Royal Thanks to:

- Papa God
- My Mom-Sandra Holcomb
- My Dad-Marvin Smith and "Momma" Carol Smith
- My Tribe of 3-my greatest accomplishment-Gage, Logan, Gabriel
- My Sisters: Tanya, Tasha, (Kathryn), and Sabrina
- Momma Alysia Renteria
- Mentor- "Momma" Linda Walker
- Mentor- "Momma" Pam Pope
- Mentor Anita Childress
- Pastor Todd and Cyndy Mooring
- Pastor Callie Shipp Gray
- Pastor Karen Edwards
- Pastor Mark and Dena Trice
- Pastor Bobbi Derry Cloyd
- Baytown Revival Center
- Hillside "Maranatha" Church
- Celebration of Life Church
- Friends Kimberly Polo and Angelica Bailey

I would not be where I am without each of you—my sincerest gratitude for believing in me when I could not believe in myself. I am so thankful God put each of you into my life. I honor each of you today. I love you.

Table of Contents

Road to Royalty

Memoires of a Pauper Traveling with the King

"Royalty!" That is not a word I would have ever used to describe myself years ago. Nope. Not in a million years. To say that I struggled to find my identity would be an understatement. Sure, I knew my name. Katherine Michelle. My dad named me. I knew my position in my immediate family. I am the third of four daughters. I have a job title, and I know what that is. I am a charge nurse. LVN. But who am I?

Through series of events, some totally out of my control and some products of my own decisions, accepting the title of *Royalty* has been extremely difficult. I carried rejection on my shoulders as a young girl until I was grown. Rejection took me through deceptive lenses. So much so, it kept me from seeing the crown He placed on my head the day I made Him my Savior.

I know I am not the only person on the planet who ever struggled to find themselves. Their true selves, who God created them to be. It took me longer than I care to admit to finally discover who I am, Whose I am, and who I am in Him. The truth is, I am learning more and more about my position in the Body of Christ and His Royal Family every day. Yet, I have not fully arrived. This book was birthed from a very dark season in my walk with Jesus heavily marked in shamed (not anymore.)

I have desired to author something to detail my journey to self-discovery - "Road to Royalty" is what I would call it. I thought to write anything regarding faith and spirituality; it must be profound, scholarly, full of scriptures, definitions, references, etc.

The creative side of me was begging to leap out onto paper. I painted several pictures, wrote several poems, and a few short stories. While finally typing them on my computer, something clicked that caused me to re-think my idea of what "Road to Royalty" should look like.

My desire and purpose for writing are 100% truth, honesty, and transparency that will be relatable to others. During my Christian walk, I believed that I was the only person to ever have experiences like mine. This was so far from the truth.

So, enclosed is a collection of short stories (actual events), poems, and artwork that I have collected over the years. I find that each one represents phases of my walk with Jesus that have ultimately played their part in my spiritual development as I travel the "Road to Royalty."

My deepest prayer for you is that the Holy Spirit will speak to you concerning similar situations/circumstances in your journey as you read through each entry. Prayerfully read through the "Think About It" entries and reflect upon your journey with Jesus. Included are short, simple prayers to pray as you journal what Holy Spirit reveals to you.

Royalty? – Hatched From an Egg

I was a gullible young girl once. I may still have a sliver of that gullibility inside me today. My almost adult children can bear witness to this, I am sure. I struggled with acceptance, value, and identity. I believe some of this is a result of a cruel joke played on me by my sisters when I was a child.

Hear my humor as I tell how rotten they were to me. (Sisters are God's built-in best friends. I love each of mine! Muah!) I am the third of four daughters born to my parents; my poor daddy was outnumbered and surrounded by estrogen. We were born four years apart, except for the older two, who are three years apart. We were all close growing up. We lived in a small wood-frame three-bedroom house. I shared a room with my baby sister.

My older sister, Tasha, was quite a role model for me. Though much shorter in stature, she was wise beyond her years with such a quiet spirit. What I admired most about her was her bank of knowledge. After all, she was my favorite teacher. If I had to guess as a child what she would be today, I would have put money on her being a teacher.

She taught me how to write my name. Primarily, my middle name because I kept spelling it M I C H E A L. She taught me how to add, subtract, fractions, word problems, etc. She was highly relevant as she explained the birds and the bees. According to this award-winning teacher of mine, I hatched from an egg.

THINK ABOUT IT...

"Outcast" is a word I know well. What labels have others placed on you that might have caused you to believe you don't belong?

Satan is the father of lies and deception. No truth can come from him. He twists the Word of God and tells half-truths.

I was born different. I was wired differently than my sisters because of who God created me to be.

Ask Papa God to show you the box in His closet. You will find that the box is empty.

You belong in His family because you are a child of God! And He made no mistake in the intricate details of who you are.

"Born Different" by K. Renteria

That's right. I hatched from an egg. "This explains so much, don't you understand. You are taller than us, your hair is darker, your skin tone is more olive-complected, plus your feet and your lips are bigger than ours. Don't you see it?"

I did see it. Everything my sister said was true. Mind you, I was young and impressionable. I would tearfully ask my parents who would deny the allegation. Anytime another difference arose between my sisters and myself, that was their response. Finally, Tasha, the scholar that she was, said to me, "Mom and Dad, don't want to hurt your feelings. I found your egg outside, right there by the mailbox under those bricks. I found you, and we put you in a box until you hatched. If you don't believe me, look in mom and dad's closet. Your eggshell is still in a box at the top of their closet."

Okay, remember I was young. I was maybe seven or eight. As much as I did not believe or want to believe that I could be an absolute outsider, the mysterious legend of my "hatching" finally got the best of me. My parents' room was the "no-zone" of our house. Getting a sneak peek into their closet had to be fast.

I don't remember the details of how I scooted past dad's security. Still, I remember standing in the dark closet on a bag of old clothes, a folded comforter, and pillows to grab ahold of the only shoebox at the top of the closet. The box fell with quite a clatter to my feet, spilling its contents. I was relieved to find there was no eggshell in the box. Unfortunately, just when I attempted to replace it all to its original location, my sisters barged in.

I could not hide the embarrassment on my face that I went looking for my eggshell. It was pretty comical for them. They got a real kick out of the whole thing. I almost wished it were true at that moment.

But the truth is, I was born different. Maybe not hatched from an eggshell, but born different, indeed. So. it turns out it's not such a bad thing after all. (PS-I love you, Tasha. I honor you today. And Sabrina, I'm sorry I tried to put you in an eggshell. I love you, baby sister.)

_____

_____

_____

_____

_____

_____

_____

_____

_____

_____

Father, show me every false label that has been placed on me. Reveal the lie I have believed that has kept me from seeing myself as You see me. Make Your nature and Your fingerprints on my life revealed to me. In Jesus Name—so be it.

Psalms 139:13-14

_____

_____

_____

_____

_____

_____

_____

_____

_____

Buckle Up - Oh, Little Girl of Faith

I see a little girl, about seven years old, walking through a field of tall, golden grass. She's out in the country, a place where she can run and play with plenty of room to explore. The sun is shining down brightly upon her. She feels free out in this field. Her smile is so bright, and her laughter is music to God's ears.

I see her now on a tire swing. She is swinging on a huge branch. The tree is enormous and has always been a place of refuge for her as a little girl. She swings back and forth, breathing in the fresh air and feeling the warm sunshine on her face. She is free. She feels loved. Does any of this make sense to you? This little girl is you.

I was at a woman's meeting when these words were spoken to me (prophetically in prayer). Standing in a circle with my peers from church, I bowed my head to receive these words. She wasn't necessarily speaking of a physical location, but I knew what she was talking about. I believe she was referring to collective moments in my childhood where I felt free in the presence of God, whether I was aware of it or not. Moments that contain the fingerprints of God, as I like to call them.

Having the benefit of hindsight, I can see those fingerprints all over my life. During the early years of my childhood, my family and I lived in a small, modest three-bedroom house on Gresham Street. I'm sure my parents believed in God, but it was not part of our family routine. Meaning, we didn't attend church together, read the Bible, bless our food, or do any other things that families typically do together to include Jesus in their day-to-day activities. But there was a church just about on every corner, it seemed. One of which was a small Nazarene Church. Because we lived so close, Mom and Dad let us girls walk together to this quaint little church.

And it offered boredom relief for my sisters and me on many Sunday mornings and summer breaks for Vacation Bible School. There were several Easter Sundays and Christmas services we attended as well. I can't recall the first time I ever walked those halls or the last. But there are other specific things I can still see in my mind today. The church had a large steeple on the outside, and inside the sanctuary were rows of wooden pews with no padding. The back of each pew had built-ins for the hymnals. At the front of the sanctuary were the tall wooden podium and a large church piano. I can still hear the songs we'd sing in Sunday school and the congregation as we sang from the hymnals.

Father open my eyes. Bring to my remembrance the moment You marked me for Yourself. In Jesus Name, so be it!

Ephesians 1:4

One Sunday morning, when I was about seven years old, my sisters and I were seated in the sanctuary, all dressed in our Sunday dresses. As usual, I sat quietly in the middle of my two older sisters (probably to keep my younger sister and me from fighting). I listened intently as the pastor closed his sermon and the piano began to play. As the pastor was giving the altar call, my little brown eyes were leaking tears down my cheeks. There was an urgency building up on the inside of me I'd never felt before. I felt drawn to the altar. I couldn't explain it. Finally, I stood up and scooted past my sisters. They whispered at me as I squeezed around them, "Where are you going? Sit down. I'm going to tell dad." To their surprise and my own, I made my way up the aisle toward the podium. I vaguely remember the Pastor as he met this little girl right there at the altar. "Blessed are the children of God."

On the way home after church, my sisters questioned me about why I got up out of my seat. While I had no real answers for any of them, I didn't need any. At that moment, I was being reeled in like a small fish in the vast ocean. Simple as that.

And soon after being reeled in, I'd be back home and changed into my play clothes for another afternoon of summer boredom.

_____

_____

_____

_____

_____

_____

_____

_____

_____

_____

_____

_____

_____

_____

_____

_____

_____

_____

_____

_____

_____

Four Flat Tires – And a Field of Potholes

I could summarize much of my life in several sad-sap-cry-me-a-river country songs. But, of course, I could ultimately spare everyone the sad details (and myself the embarrassment of sharing said details). Still, for enlightenment to you (reader)-I will indulge.

The devil doesn't play fair-period. He is not on our side. He does not want us to know who we are or how much God loves us. Like many others, rejection became my constant companion at a very, very young age. I have so many memories to choose from, ranging from my parents, sisters, childhood friends and classmates, crushes, boyfriends, a crazy ex-girlfriend, and an ex-husband. I could write an entire book on the devastating effects of rejection. As I was talking with my oldest son on the matter once, he said, "Wow, mom, you have been attacked your whole life in the area of LOVE, haven't you?"

Yep, and to sum it all up, here is one of my oldest memories that helps put it into perspective for me. I was about four. Our home had an old white, detached wooden garage. The front part (facing the street) was big enough for one vehicle and had a workspace/storage area partition. As for us kids, the garage was off-limits.

I remember having company that day, and all the kids were playing out in the yard, going back and forth in and out of the house. As the evening approached, I wandered into the back part of the garage. It was dark in there, not much natural light, with cobwebs and rat traps scattered everywhere.

I could hear one of the adults begin calling all the kids back inside the house. I remember one clear thought, "I wonder if they will even know I'm gone." I climbed onto the bottom cabinet and lifted myself to the top cabinet. I tucked myself in the shadows, and I waited. And I waited some more.

For a young child, a few minutes felt like days. But soon, the streetlights came on. The sky was turning orange, and I could hear someone calling my name. I remember being happy that I was missed, but I remained hidden. It was almost as if I asked myself, "How hard will they search? Will they be upset if no one

Father, help me to identify every pair of deceptive lenses that have caused me to see in myself anything but what You say I am. Give me Your lenses to see myself through. What do You have to say about me?

Ephesians 2:5-6

finds me? What lengths will anyone go to to find the girl that does not matter." At one point, the door opened briefly, and I saw someone glance in and walk out.

Of course, after no one came back in and I was left in the dark, I surrendered.

_____

_____

_____

_____

_____

_____

_____

_____

_____

Operating the Radio-Oh, No Ma'am

When we were kids, visiting Grandma and Grandpa in Livingston was a treat. For years, a handful of us grandkids would spend an entire week with them. These are special memories for me. They created imprints when I wasn't looking.

Grandma and Grandpa built their home in the seventies. I imagine their idea was to create a legacy for their children and their grandchildren. Good job, Grandpa, you did well.

The summers overflowed with great memories. Seven fun-filled days with our cousins tromping around in the woods, racing barefoot on the dirt roads, and pretending to drive the tractor. The smell of coffee brewing before the sun ever came up. Grandpa looked out over the backfield, watching the deer while sipping his first cup. Quiet chatter between him and grandma at the table. The smell of bacon or sausage wafting through the house and waking up to grandma sitting in her chair reading her bible. Her old, black leather bible that held together with duct tape. Even her gathering all her "chicks" at her feet to teach us. It may have felt like a scolding sometimes, but it is still one of her greatest attributes.

One thing she said stuck with me, "Kathy, God called you to be in this world, not of it." I'm not going to lie; I did not want to hear that. But those words stuck with me until this very day. I can still hear her words as if it were just yesterday.

I had a relationship with a female in my early twenties that lasted about two years. In the beginning, it was like putting on a new pair of shoes, though she was not the

THINK ABOUT IT...

I am so thankful for the hand of God that pulled me out of this relationship.

I needed His rescue whether I knew it or not. The truth is, I was spiritually sick.

As I reflect on His goodness towards me, I can't help but to be wrecked by how patient He was in His pursuit of my heart.

How has God in His mercy rescued you when you weren't looking?

How did that rescue play out in the next chapter of your life?

first female I was intimate with. I guess I can say it felt like my way of fighting back at all the boys who deeply hurt me from my past. Ignorance may be bliss, but I knew better. "Kathy, God called you to be in this world, not of it."

By the end, the relationship turned violent, degrading, and shameful in the worst way. I left her and our apartment in shambles. I cried the whole way back to my hometown. I did not want it to end, but I knew it was time.

In retrospect I could see God picking me up by the back of the neck and removing me from that relationship. Enough was enough! Oh no, He was ensuring that I was in the world and not of it.

God had His work cut out for Him. I'm glad He knew what He was doing. A few months later, I became pregnant.

_____
_____
_____
_____
_____
_____
_____
_____
_____
_____
_____
_____
_____
_____
_____
_____
_____
_____

Father, I thank You for Your rescue plan You have set in motion. Whether I knew or know it or not, I need rescue from my own brokenness. I accept your rescue that brings me closer to You. In Jesus Name, so be it.

Jeremiah 29:11

_____
_____
_____

Start Your Engines - Just Do It!

I walked through our trailer park towards the office. Debbie, the office manager, was a kind woman who I'd come to know a little after she and her husband first took the position. She was about ten years older than me, soft-spoken, and very wise. Her spiritual antenna, I would quickly learn, was tuned directly into the heart of Jesus.

Our family lived there a couple of years before Debbie and her husband moved in. The mailboxes sat right outside the office building, so I would run into her from time to time while checking the mail. Plus, I always paid our rent in person. I'd often go inside to find her reading, listening to a teaching tape, or simply enjoying soft worship music. She would attempt to strike up a friendly conversation, but I rarely indulged. Until, of course, my world began to fall apart at the seams. Then I was all ears.

My marriage was falling apart, and I knew it. For several weeks, I could feel a distance between us. I couldn't put a pin on it, but it was there, staring me in the face. Once I finally confronted him, he was honest enough to admit that he felt the same way. Except he was considering divorce as the final answer. I knew the power of prayer, but I did not have a personal relationship with Jesus.

Now, we all know every excellent sprinter starts somewhere, right? But, just before the flag drops, each contestant lines up nice and orderly at the starting line. They've done all the hard work to prepare. They've surrendered to grueling fitness training, nutrition coaching, and hours of practice and pre-runs with their eyes on the prize. Now, everyone must start somewhere and be willing to put in the work when they do. I could say the delay on my part to get serious was because I was never picked first in gym class for any sporting event.

THINK ABOUT IT...

He chose me before I chose Him. Even though I was buried in a muck of rejection, that truth was louder than lies.

He chose me. With that in mind, I had to decide. Will I decide to live my life in total surrender to Him? Will I partner with Him to walk out His perfect will, plan, and purpose for my life? Or will I keep traveling a road that is sure to end in tragedy?

For someone as headstrong as myself, surrendering was hard. But I am so thankful I stepped to the starting line.

Remember, your journey is a process.

What have you decided?

Of course, I'm kidding. The truth is, I did not understand the requirement to throw my hat in the ring in the first place. I'm not talking about believing Jesus is the Son of the Living God who died for my sins so that I may go to Heaven. We all know that is our invitation to join the race. No, I'm talking about what it takes to go from there - Surrender. I attempted many times during my childhood and adolescent teenage years, and again, in my young adult years. Sadly, "surrender" was not a part of my vocabulary. Not yet anyway.

I stepped into the office to pay what I could for that month's rent. My face was still red, and my eyes were puffy. We discussed the rent and other things while she prepared my receipt, and soon enough, we started talking about Jesus. I was finally ready to talk. I said, "I can feel Him pulling on me. I can't explain it. I don't have the words for it, except I hear Him say surrender, but I don't know how to do that. How do I surrender? What does that look like?"

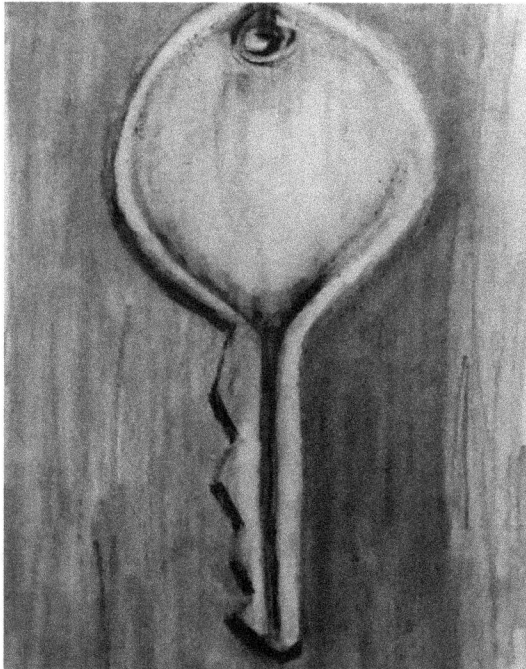

Charcoal "Key"

Debbie looked at me with such kindness as she held my hand. Her response floored me. "It's easy, sweetheart; you just do it." WHAT?! Really? It's that easy?" I scoffed on the inside. I walked away from that conversation feeling quite baffled and disappointed. "I can't believe I asked her how to surrender to God, and the flipping answer I got was, "JUST DO IT!"

Un-believe-able!!!" I continued in my mental rant. "Wow!"

Well, the truth of the matter is, it is that easy. Over the next few days, the distance grew between my husband and me. He was coming home later and later. Eventually, days would go by before he came home. His mother, Alysia, a woman I love and adore to this day, was a strong Christian woman. I finally told her what was going on between her son and me, and she immediately advised me to get into the church and pray, which I did.

I was holding on to every thread of hope I could. I can't say, though, yet that I surrendered. February 14, 2005, I picked up a Valentine's Day card and filled the inside with heartfelt words of love and sincere appreciation of him being in my life. Lord knows I loved him as much I could with what I knew about love. No, we weren't a perfect couple; but together, we stood with each of our babies shortly after they were born and dedicated them to God. I realize how insane and silly it sounds that it took so long to get to this place, but I meant it. God knows I meant it. Nothing would have made me happier if our marriage looked and operated the way God intended it to from the beginning. Unfortunately, we, I, just lacked direction. Like I said, surrender was just not a familiar concept.

He came in from work, and I handed him my card. He gave me one in return. His was a simple card with words of appreciation and gratitude signed, "Thanks for all the years. Sincerely, XOXOXO!" If anyone ever needs clarification on how I knew it was over or that Valentine's Day was the day my marriage was a dead one, reread it - "Thanks for all the years."

I knew what it meant. My heart was tearing into a million tiny little pieces right there in my living room while he showered and readied himself for a first date with someone new. So, what else was there left for me to do? I'm sure the presence of God was so thick in my living room that evening. And I'm also sure the angels eagerly awaited my response as the curtain dropped, and I was left to decide.

I surrendered! My husband walked out the door, and I hit the floor. I laid face down on our green carpet as I cried out to God from my toes. I wasn't begging God to make him turn around and come back home. Not entirely. I was begging God to come in, to change the girl I saw in the mirror. I hated her. For the longest time, I hated that woman.

I can say now I love and adore the woman I see today in the mirror. I am not perfect, and until I get to heaven, Jesus and I will always be working on

Father, I step boldly to the starting line with the full knowledge I must start somewhere. You chose me long before I chose You. Today, I chose to partner with You. Let's start our race together. In Jesus name, so be it.

1 Corinthians 9:24

something. But, if anybody were to ask me now, I have to say, "Yes, I guess surrender is that easy. You just do it."

_____

_____

_____

_____

_____

_____

_____

_____

_____

_____

_____

_____

_____

_____

_____

_____

_____

_____

_____

Gas Mileage - Give it Back

When I was a kid, I visited a Pentecostal church from time to time with my sister's best friend, Kathryn (who lived next door). It was there I was first exposed to the Holy Ghost and all His mysteriousness. As a child of eight or nine, I can assure you, I did not understand any of it. The concept was so strange that two other girls I met in Sunday school (who were visiting my neighbor) and I innocently played "Holy Ghost and Fire" in my backyard after church.

The three of us laughed as we pretended to be skirted Pentecostal women at the altar receiving "the fire," Yes...it was quite a scene. We jumbled words together in pretense as we shook our bodies violently. We were having so much fun. That is until Kathryn's mom, dad, Brother Tommy, and Sister Anna came running out of their house and rounded up my two friends for a scolding. Kids. They are cute, right?

Some years later, as a teen, I returned to that Pentecostal church. The pastor, Sister Harvey, prayed for me to receive the baptism of the Holy Spirit. I remember only one thing from this snippet of my life. I felt a surge of supernatural electricity running through me and tears uncontrollably falling as I received. I returned home that afternoon to my parents and sisters, and life went on.

Yes, life went on. With ups and downs. With a few good choices and hundreds of foolish ones. Life went on as Jesus chased after me, and I ran. Life went on. Until that is when I finally fell face down in surrender to Him. The love of Jesus was being poured out thick all over me. My eyes were finally opened to Truth. The scales of deception were falling off at every turn. I had a burning on the inside and an urgency to tell the world about the Love of Jesus the Christ. And then I received a wild invitation. One I couldn't

THINK ABOUT IT...

When I received the Baptism of the Holy Spirit and received my new prayer language, my prayer life received a jumpstart.

I began to "see" and "feel" the Heart of God as I fervently prayed.

Having the understanding I do now makes the importance of both praying in my own understanding and in the Holy Spirit.

Why do you suppose the enemy tries so hard to keep us as believers from receiving and using our new prayer language when we are baptized in the Holy Spirit?

What is your greatest experience while using your new prayer language?

say "no" to.

I remember going to my mother-in-law's house to tell her all about this wild invitation I had just received. "I was lying in my bed, not thinking about anything. Out of nowhere, I saw this flash like a picture being taken. It was me. I was standing in front of a huge audience of women with a microphone in my hand. I was preaching with power and authority. I even gasped like, "not me?" I can't do that! Are You sure? Then it happened again, but the next time I heard clearly, "I will be with you!"

Oh, the excitement we both felt right then! She smiled so big as she confided, "I knew it! I knew ministry was in you all along! You need the Holy Ghost to help you along!" As she went on to explain, I understood the importance. Thus, I was first in line at the altar to receive the following Sunday. With both hands raised to Jesus, I closed my eyes and asked Him for the Gift of the Baptism of the Holy Spirit. I asked Him for and thanked Him in advance for my new prayer language. That familiar surge of electricity ran through my body, and again, tears ran uncontrollably as the first three syllables of my new prayer language flowed out of my mouth. (Still to this day, I love to watch someone else receive this gift. It gets me every time.)

After leaving the altar, the instruction I received was just as important as the instructions I received just before. I received a pamphlet written by our Pastor. In short, he explained that Satan does not want believers equipped with a new prayer language. It is powerful. It is Holy Spirit praying through us. It is a direct communication line between the Father and me. And the devil will use the same tactics he always uses to disarm the saints from using this new gift. Lies.

Yes. Lies. The devil will use lies to keep us from using this new language. And it didn't take long for those lies to start coming after my new language. "It's not real." "See, you can't even understand what you're saying." "He didn't give you that." These lies relentlessly aimed and fired at my new gift. So much to the point where I would open my mouth to pray, and nothing would come out. Over and over again, one after another. Lie after lie. As hard as I tried, nothing would come out. Then I started to get angry. Like really, really, angry. If ever there were an appropriate time to cuss out the devil, this was it. I finally had enough. I was so desperate.

I stomped my way down the hallway, went to my room, and slammed the door. I knelt at the foot of my bed and prayed. "Heavenly Father, I know You gave me that gift. It is mine. You did not take it back. It is not gone. I have the gift; You gave to me. And right now, by the power of the blood of Jesus Christ in me, Satan, I DEMAND you to take your hands off my gift and give it back!" I could say that the trailer shook as I prayed, but I may be embellishing a little. Regardless, what came next was no surprise, a steady flow of my new prayer language. There it was. The most beautiful syllables in the world! (cue the angelic singing and release of the doves)

I never tasted victory as sweet as it did that day. The devil picked the wrong gal to mess with.

_____

_____

_____

_____

_____

_____

Father, I ask with open hands to receive. Pour our Your Holy Spirit in me. Baptize me from the inside out with the evidence of speaking in a language I do not know. In Jesus name. So be it.

Acts 2:4

_____

_____

_____

_____

_____

_____

Sober Driving - It's a Heart Thing

I have three boys. Raising them by myself has presented some challenges. Some of them were scary. Some very strange. Some hysterical. They've done some pretty silly things, and I'm sure they would not be happy if I shared them. Luckily, this isn't about them. This is all about me and is 100% true. It's stories like this one that make me grateful that Papa God is a very, very, very, very (did I say "very"?) patient Father as we grow and learn.

Before inviting Jesus into my heart, I had a hobby. Um, okay, not a hobby, but an addiction. While some say marijuana is non-addictive, I would have to agree to disagree. I got high in the morning. I got high in the afternoon. I got high before bed. I got high when I was happy. I got high when I was sad. I got high when I was angry. I got high when I was not. Every occasion was an occasion to roll up a doobie and toke it up. I can recall many situations where I had a legitimate reason to feel wronged or hurt, "packing-a-bowl" always seemed to make it all better.

I admire those who have testimonies of immediate deliverance from drug addiction almost instantaneous upon salvation. It is beautiful, and I am in awe of the power of the Blood of Jesus that breaks the chains of addiction. I'm sure that could have happened for me, but it didn't. I was saved and on my way to heaven, but I was stubborn and had a hard time serving Ms. Mary Jane her eviction papers.

Friends, it gets worse. I would go to church on Sunday morning or a Wednesday night and worship my little heart out. I would come home still fired up with excitement. So fired up, I had to share my new revelations with my

THINK ABOUT IT...

It was very difficult for me in the very beginning of my faith walk knowing that this and other bad habits was taking so long to break off.

I understand now that God was not much interested in my bad habits, but the root of them.

After I acknowledged my error, I received His tender mercy. He is a loving God, and only wants to heal our hurts.

If you asked God to show you your heart, what might you find?

Are there things or people or attitudes even, you reach for when you are feeling unsettled?

What do you hear the Father say to you about it?

friends. My friends that I bought my pot from. I would go to their house, sit in their living room, spew out all my new spiritual treasures (with genuine excitement and enthusiasm), all the while puffing on and passing around a big ole fat joint. (Here is where I hang my head in embarrassment.)

Picture this if you can. I come home from church; this little southern bell of a woman donned in her best Sunday morning attire. I am standing in my friends' doorway, smiling ear to ear with these words on my lips, "Guys, Church this morning was so freaking awesome! Let me tell ya'll what I learned today! But, first, does anybody have a Zig-Zag?"

Slowly though, things started to change. I would buy (in small amounts) some pot, smoke maybe a half a joint, and get so convicted I would flush it down the toilet. Then a few days later, I would find myself doing it again. Luckily in those early weeks after salvation, the Love Light of Jesus shining down on me kept me running hard after Him. One Friday afternoon, I listened to a teaching CD by a prominent minister who I greatly admire. One thing she said during one of her teachings that caught my attention and sparked some bravery was, "If you want to be brave, I mean really brave, ask God to show you your heart. And be ready because He will." Well, that was all I needed to hear. I wanted to be brave. I wanted to show God that I meant business. "Okay, God show me my heart."

It wasn't a day later that something (I can't even tell you what it was anymore, I don't remember) sent me running to my room, a crying mess to light up. I laid there in my room, high as a kite, for a few minutes staring at the ceiling fan above my bed, watching it circle, thinking about how dirty it was—then thinking about the rest of the room and how bad it needed to be cleaned. I started to chuckle as I realized just how high I must have been to waste so many minutes staring at a dusty ceiling fan. But suddenly, out of nowhere-Wham! There it is. An image that would flash and cause any feeling of intoxication to disappear immediately.

"Show me, my heart God." I heard in my voice. I saw a quick picture of me running to an ambulance with my inner pain and lighting up like taking medicine. In that brief glimpse, I felt the sting of knowing I walked right past the Great Physician who could heal it all.

Now, talk about deliverance. I got it that day.

_____

_____

_____

_____

_____

Father, I ask You to show me areas in my life that I have not fully given to You. I trade every addiction that I have used as a source of comfort for You, The Comforter. In Jesus name, so be it.

Psalms 51:10

_____

_____

_____

_____

_____

_____

_____

_____

_____

_____

_____

_____

_____

Unlawful Passengers - She's Gotta Go-Go

THINK ABOUT IT...

I know God understood my heart in my request to Him concerning my friend. And I have no doubts of His love for each one of us.

As a parent myself, I also understand the Fathers heart toward us. He knows what is best for us at all times.

It hurts sometimes when He asks us to lay things, and relationships on the altar, even if we know it is for our own good.

Who or what have you laid on the altar that you knew was in your best interest to do so?

Where do you think you would be today if you had not obeyed?

"You ready? I'm going to pray for you, and God will talk to you about some things. You ready?" Pastor asked. "Yes, sir," I replied. "I'm ready." I was at a singles ministry meeting at our church, and the message that night touched on things we needed to lay on the altar. Not that Holy Spirit was showing me anything specific I needed to lay down. I just had an unction. So, I made my way up to the front to receive prayer at the end of the message. I have no idea what he prayed or how exactly he prayed it. All I remember is his hand on my forehead, falling backward and getting a rather specific word of instruction.

I had a friend (who I will call) Lynn, whom I met before my Christian life, who lived across the street. She and I had a lot in common at the time, though she was several years older than me. We both had three children, three sons, to be exact. Neither one of us was educated. We both shared an affinity for certain four-letter words, and we both smoked Marlboro cigarettes and used marijuana regularly and daily. After my marriage fell apart, we also had our single status in common as well. Shortly after I got saved, Lynn made the statement, "Your gonna be just like me."

I witnessed her struggle with singleness, financial hardships, depression, and cocaine over the past few years. Thankfully, I knew the power of words, so that declaration was disarmed immediately after hearing them. I can't convince anyone that our friendship was a healthy one, but I knew Lynn for quite some time, and I was privy to all her unfortunate experiences. I genuinely cared about her. I remember praying once, "I don't want her to be left behind. Use me, Lord. Use me to bring her to You."

Lynn had some very rough edges, and she let me know early on she wanted nothing to do with Jesus. She never blew up at me when I talked about my new life, but the undertone was present. I knew it would be wise to tread lightly. She lost her mother at an early age in life to cancer and was angry with God. She was in and out of numerous sexual relationships, but drug addiction was her only constant driving force. By the time I moved out of our neighborhood, she had moved into another apartment and another relationship. Two of her boys moved out to escape the madness. Though we were not as close as we used to be, I made sure to check on her a few times a month.

As I lay on the floor of my church, a single image flashed before my closed eyelids, followed by three simple words. It was a picture of my friend and the words, "Leave her alone." That was it. Simple instruction. "Leave her alone." I have heard several times during my Christian walk that delayed obedience is disobedience. But I was still a baby Christian, and I was not familiar with that concept. (But for the mercy and the Grace of God.)

A few weeks passed after this meeting, and I was on my way home from nursing school. One of my teachers informed me that my name was submitted for a summer scholarship, and it was granted. Of course, this was great news, and I was so excited. I could not wait to tell someone, and Lynn's apartment was on my way home.

She answered the door and invited me in. We briefly exchanged words, but she quickly excused herself to go to the bathroom. Her apartment was small, dimly lit, and every table surface was decorated with empty beer cans and ashtrays. I stared at the familiar pictures of her children hanging on the wall. They were not little anymore, and I wondered where they were. I sat in her living room, and as the minutes passed, I increasingly felt uneasy. Finally, I got up and knocked on her hollow bathroom door.

"Lynn, are you okay?" I asked as I tapped on the door.

"Yeah. I'll be out in a minute." Lynn replied. "I just bought some heroin, and I want to finish it all before Mike gets home. He doesn't know I bought it and will be ticked if he finds out, so I've got to get rid of it."

In all the time I'd known Lynn, her doing heroin was new to me. I knew she had a cocaine addiction some years before, but she always said needles gave her "the heebie-jeebies." I could hardly believe what I was hearing. My heart was saddened to know my friend was sticking needles in her arms.

I could hear her struggle behind the bathroom door with whatever it was she was doing.

"Come out already, Lynn." I pleaded.

"Just a sec. I told you. I just wanna get this all in. I can't find the vein," Lynn replied. I was not familiar with heroin, heroin use, or anything else heroin related. The only thing I knew about the heroine is that some overdose on it. My imagination began to run wild with pictures of paramedics, police officers, caskets, and the like. I tried to open the door, but it was locked. "No! Don't come in here. Just go sit in the living room."

Truthfully, I just wanted to go home, but I retreated to the sofa to wait it out. I couldn't hear anything from the bathroom, and I knew I had no business being in her apartment. Minutes ticked by. Twenty-five minutes, to be exact. Finally, I returned to the door, put my hand up, and quietly prayed, "Lord, bring her out of this bathroom alive, and I will leave her alone. I get it. Please bring her out."

Just then, I could hear more rustling inside, and she opened the door. I made some fast, polite small talk, hugged her neck, and I left.

That was over ten years ago, and I haven't seen Lynn except on the streets. I ran into her at a gas station while on a ministry treasure hunt. She looked tired and worn down. We exchanged pleasantries, but as she walked away, I knew she was the same Lynn I last saw in her apartment. I still pray and trust God for her salvation when I think about her, but I can't help but thank God for His simple instruction all those years ago. I don't know where I would be right now had He not told me, "Leave her alone."

Father, I ask You to reveal anything that has the potential for our relational ruin. Give me the strength to follow through with obedience in laying it on the altar. I understand You always have my best interest at heart with intent for me to follow You. In Jesus name, so be it.

Luke 14:26

Two and Ten- The Gift

It was a good sermon that Sunday morning. As per my new usual, I made my way up to the altar at the end of the message. In my Sunday best, with cheap non-waterproof mascara streaked down my cheeks, I soaked up my tears and snot as the prayer partner said, "Amen." I was a hot mess of a woman those first few months after salvation. I jokingly tell people I should have changed my mailing address to my "campout spot" at the altar. It seemed like every message I heard on Wednesdays and Sundays was aimed directly at my heart to untangle the mess I spent years becoming.

Between prayers of repentance, prayers and supplication for emotional healing, and financial provision for my family were also pleas to see the deepest of my desires to come to pass. Desires I clung hard and fast to as if my next breath depended on seeing them come to pass. I was unaware that I had my nails dug in, clenched to, and unwilling to give them to the One who could do anything with them.

I remember the compassion I felt at that moment with the prayer partner. Her eyes were so kind. Her voice was so soothing. It reminds me of the labor nurse that worked with me when I was delivering my oldest son. With her soft voice saying, "I know it hurts, breath out slowly, it will all be over in 5, 4, 3, 2... there you go.... good job" as she gently rubbed my contracting belly. When my mom tried to do it, I snapped at her. (I am sorry, Momma!)

THINK ABOUT IT...

Any road we travel that leads us unto the arms of Jesus is a good one.

I came to Jesus a broken mess who just wanted to:

1) be able to love myself again

2) have my marriage restored to a healed and Godly marriage.

While a lot of prayers have been answered, some were not. I had to learn to trust His heart and intentions toward me.

What are you trusting God for?

Do you trust God's heart for you? For His 100% perfect will for your life?

What might His gift to you look like if you traded your will for His?

Original charcoal sketch "The Gift" K Renteria

I do not remember her exact prayer over me that morning, but I remember her words after. She brushed my hair back and wiped away my mascara mess and tears. "You know, I see Papa holding His hands out with this HUGE present, beautifully wrapped with ribbons and a big bow with your name on it. And He is holding it out to you. I hear Him saying,

"If you let go of what you think you want, I will give you something so much better. He designed it and wrapped it Himself. He cannot wait to give it to you." I

Father, give me Your vision to see the plans for my life. Help me trade my understanding for Yours as my future is unveiled. In Jesus name, so be it.

Proverbs 3:5-6

can feel His excitement and anticipation. It's all for you." Although her voice was soothing to an aching spirit, I did not understand totally at that moment what He was trying to say. Was I distracted by the threat of a snot bubble or the stain of my mascara on my dress? I'm not sure, but I am thankful. His words to me are still alive today.

I dwelt on those words for YEARS as little by little I surrendered my will to His. It is a big, beautiful present where I am only beginning to see underneath the paper and ribbons. I feel at times like a little girl again ripping into the "Santa" present under the tree.

I always dreamed of traveling, and today I travel. I always dreamed of teaching, and today I teach. I always dreamed of writing, and today I am writing. I always dreamed of making beautiful art, and today I create beautiful art. I used to be afraid of boldness, but today I am bold for Christ.

And I am still peeling back the paper and only looking at the box!

Fueled by Faith

I am walking along a dirt road. It seems to be a somewhat familiar dirt road. Maybe it is the dirt road I walked on as a young girl when I visited Grandma and Grandpa in Livingston. It sure feels comforting looking down at the orange dirt under my bare feet. There I am, surrounded by tall pines swaying back and forth in the wind.

The sunlight is peeking through with broken shadows on the ground. I feel so free as I walk along this dirt road taking in all the splendor of Mother Nature and the sweet melody of peace. I seemed to be dancing as I walked. Unabated excitement I could not explain began to build as my awkward trot on the dirt road began to pick up its intensity until I was running freely. I had moments where I felt sure the wind would pick me up and carry me over the trees. If I could see my freckled face, it would have the biggest smile ever worn plastered all over it.

Until I tripped and on what I don't know, I can feel the cold dirt on my cheek and the burn on my hands and knees. I can see with great clarity as I lifted my brow to look at the road full of potholes, rocks, and the grass median as I tried to collect myself and remove the small pebbles from my flesh.

I tried to push myself up to an upright position, but gravity laid across my back. I could take only a few lurching steps before I was back on my knees. Several times, I struggled to stand upright again but was met with the same result. I became frustrated as time and time again I would begin a lurched run only to land a painful fall. Finally, I stretched out on the dirt road, clenching the grass, crying out to God, "Help me! I don't

THINK ABOUT IT...

I feel silly sometimes when I reflect on this dream because it took me so long to ask Him what it meant.

I realize I was young and spiritually undeveloped, but I can't help but to wonder where I would be today if I had the revelation I do now.

It prompted me to ask:

How does my faith look to You?

Is it steady?

Help me to develop my faith skills as I learn to walk to with You.

understand!" And then I'd wake up. I repeatedly had this dream throughout my childhood until I was thirty.

What does it mean? What have You tried to show me?

"Is it so difficult to understand? This is your faith. Gravity is an assault on your faith. Get back up again. Every time you fall, get back up again. You will walk again. You will run again. You will dance again. You will soar."

Father, I ask that You help me identify and overcome any struggle I may have as I learn to walk by faith. I understand learning to walk without natural vision is a process and I am ready to do so with You. In Jesus name, so be it.

2 Corinthians 5:7

_____

_____

_____

_____

_____

_____

_____

_____

_____

_____

_____

_____

Car-seats – Hold Me, Daddy!

I sat in the car in front of the house one Sunday after church. Maybe I stayed behind to fix my make-up. After all, I did tend to melt into a hot, heaping mess as I sang my heart out to Jesus with the rest of the choir. Maybe I stayed behind to finish listening to the song that was playing on the radio. Or perhaps I stayed behind in my car because I knew all too well the second, I went inside, I'd have three little boys hanging all over me looking for lunch, and I just wasn't in the mood to deal with it right at that moment.

There could be many reasons I chose to sit outside by myself in the heat of the day, but it was most likely to have ten minutes of deep, intimate, uninterrupted prayer. This Sunday afternoon was not the first time I used my car as my prayer closet. I don't remember what song was playing. I don't know what words came out in prayer, but I remember this moment clearly as it marks the moment that I understood "Abba."

My prayer language flowed sweetly as my heart focused on His heart for me and my heart for Him. Images played in my mind as I felt a nudge to run into the arms of my daddy, but I couldn't. I could sense His arms held out to me as I was about to take my first steps as a toddler, but I couldn't. I hesitated, and by the time I cut the engine off and got out of the car, my heart was pained that I could not. I might as well have been that toddler; except I just fell and was now feeling the sting.

I did not even get to open the small wooden gate to go into the yard before changing my mind and getting back into my car. I didn't put the key into the ignition. I just sat there in my car and continued to pray in my prayer

THINK ABOUT IT...

As a child, I knew my dad loved me. As you will read through the text, I know I wore some deceptive lenses when it came to equating "God in Heaven" and "God my Father."

Sometimes our perception of God is mirrored by our experiences.

Why is it important to God that we see Him as a loving Father?

language until I could see His face again. When I did, I could see His arms stretched out as to say, "Raise your hands, let me hold You." I could see it. I could feel a deep yearning to take that step to let Him hold me. His eyes were kind. His hold on me was firm but loving. I was home. I sat weeping in the car, "Hold me, Daddy. Hold me, Daddy." I could feel His tender and proud response. This was the first time I called Him "Daddy."

_____

_____

_____

_____

_____

_____

_____

_____

_____

_____

_____

_____

_____

_____

Engine Lights - Not Ready

I had a very vivid dream over a decade ago. It was a dream I will never forget. A dream that was packed with details and layer upon layer of meaning and significance. I was still what I would consider being a toddler in my walk with Christ at the time; however, it is applicable at every stage of growth.

I was a member of the choir at the church I was planted in at the time. In the dream, I arrived early to church one Sunday morning for choir practice. Walking into the church, I was stunned at the atmosphere as I entered. It was my church, but it was as if I were walking into a bar in the 1970s. The place was dimly lit with a strobe light in the entranceway. Several folks passed by without giving me a second glance.

The air was stale, and it looked like cigarette smoke was wafting through the place as idle chatter and laughter filled the silence. Everyone was dressed in their bar-room attire, and nobody seemed to be aware of the fact we were in the House of God. I walked around the room, taking note of what I was seeing. I was so confused and felt so out of place as I went from room to room looking for somebody I recognized.

Nobody made eye contact with me. I felt so uneasy as I looked around. I finally concluded I was in the right place, but I was just super early. With that, I decided I had a little bit more time to get ready for the morning service. I could leave, get ready, and come back. I exited the sanctuary and made my way to my car.

The scene then flips to me, pulling into a relative's (no idea who) driveway. Immediately, I noticed several other cars parked along the street and in the yard. When I stepped inside, the place was abuzz with several women scurrying around, hurrying to get dressed. One was putting on her makeup, and another was curling her hair. One was trying on different outfits, and another was putting on her hose. I walked toward the back of the house. One lady exited the bathroom, fresh out of the shower. Suddenly, I realized that the stench of earlier events was stuck on my skin, and my clothing was in disarray. I asked if I could take a shower as well, and they welcomed me to do so.

I stripped down naked and stepped into a shower stall with opaque glass doors. The warm water sprayed down on me as I lathered up and bathed. Steam filled the bathroom, which now resembled a lady's locker room. As I bathed, I took extra care to wash every fold diligently. Rinsing off, I looked down at my chest and noticed I was still wearing my bra. I was initially a little embarrassed that I forgot to take it off in the first place. I removed it and swung it over the top of the sliding door. Continuing to bathe, I smiled a little, thinking it was, after all, a little humorous.

Then, I realized I was still wearing my panties. Any smile I was wearing quickly disappeared as I thought, "Wait a minute. I know I took those off before I got in." I took them off and threw those over the top, too, and began to wash my body frantically. Scrubbing hard, I rewashed my arms and chest, but again, there was my bra, panties, and socks. I kept taking them off, and they kept reappearing. I was freaking out-thinking; it feels like a satanic attack. Finally, I turned the water off and got out. One of the ladies handed me a huge white towel and a white bathrobe to cover myself. Sopping wet and wrapped in a bathrobe, I ran out of the bathroom and through the house. I was overtaken by feeling an urgent need for prayer.

The scene flips again back to the church. I am still soaking wet and wrapped in a robe. This time, the church looks like a wedding is about to take place. The lighting was perfect. Bundles of gorgeous white roses decorated the room. There was soft music playing in the background. The women (from my aunt's house) were all dressed, and I recognized many of them as our church leaders. They all looked gorgeous as they stood there adorned in beautiful satin and lace, white wedding gowns.

Their hair was perfectly curled, as their diamonds, pearls, and gold jewelry glistened in the soft white lighting. Their smiles were highlighted with lipstick and gloss. They looked perfect, and I was in a bathrobe. I could sense the excitement in the room building as the ceremony was about to begin. I became frantic inside knowing, screaming in my inner voice, "I am not ready!" I scurried around the room, approaching every lady I recognized, those who I knew who could pray, whose prayer I knew reached the throne of God. I begged them to help me to get ready. But to my dismay, everyone I approached blankly looked at me and brushed past as to say, "I don't have time to help you." I could hear, "Here comes the Bride" beginning to play in the background. The sense of urgency was reaching its peak. I was shaking inside. Sheer panic was taking over. Finally sensing defeat, I crumbled to the floor and started to cry.

My audible weeping awakened me. I had tears running down onto my soaked pillow. While there are many things I glean from this dream, it serves as a good reminder. A reminder that I am responsible for making myself ready for the Bridegroom. Yes, growth is a process as I co-labor with the Holy Spirit, but it will not magically happen independently. And yes, prayer is good and all, but there's no one whose prayers can do the hard work of getting ready for me. Once it's too late, it's too late. Time to get busy, and the time is now.

_____

_____

Father, I thank You so much that I am Your bride. I trust that as we partner together, I can continually be found doing my part in making myself ready for Your return. Continue to teach me, change me, and fellowship with me until that day comes. In Jesus name, so be it.

Matthew 25:1-13

_____

_____

_____

_____

GPS - PS: I Love You

"Kathy, are you going tonight?"

"No," I replied as I pulled the covers over my head and turned over.

"So, are you going to throw a hissy fit and blame God now? Is that it?" Alysia snapped. She stood there at the door a few seconds before closing my door in retreat.

I laid under the covers as tears continued to stream down my cheeks. My kids, who were seven, four, and one at the time, had just come home from a weekend with their dad. After listening to their accounts of all the fun they had, I made my way to my room for a tearful retreat in bed. Images played in my mind of my children spending the weekend with their dad and his new live-in girlfriend like a bad movie. The thought haunted me that not only did my soon-to-be ex-husband now love someone else, but my children did also too.

"Father, this hurts so bad! Do you even care?" I thought silently to myself as I continued to sob.

In retrospect, I realize I was pouting like a child. But the wound was fresh, bleeding, and too close for comfort. I was newly separated from my husband of seven years, and the sting of losing him worsened because it was to another woman. At that moment, I felt I lost everything.

I had no job. No money. No skills. My home, once known to my little family, was rolled right out of the trailer park. The kids and I were now living with his mother. Do not get me wrong; she was the biggest blessing to me to at the time. She took us in when no one else would. I was newly born again but tragically broken. I needed a lot of guidance, prayer, and a whole lot of grace. She was there.

THINK ABOUT IT...

Yes, I was throwing a pity party. Yes, I was the only one in attendance. But God knew the pain I was feeling.

He is a good Daddy and wants His daughters to know He is here for us, He hears us, and wants nothing more than for His daughters to know He will do anything to let us know that.

What did your "PS" note say to you?

"Get dressed. I already bought our tickets. It will do you good to get out," Alice said in a last attempt to get me out of my funk.

Of course, she was right. I threw the covers off and got the kids and myself dressed to go to our church's annual lady's dinner party.

Once I hurried the kids to the nursery, I made my way to the gym, arranged with several tables creatively decorated by a table sponsor. The idea was that each table would be an artistic display of scripture. Looking around the room, I admired the creativity.

One was decorated with what looked like driftwood. The theme was "Ship-wrecked Faith."

Another was a baby shower theme to announce the birth of Jesus.

Another with fishnets and tackle, I think you get the idea.

Our table was arranged with Legos, as in "Fitly joined together." Our meals were served as the speaker for the night came out to deliver the message, and to this day, I have no idea what that message was because my eyes were so fixated on the table adjacent to ours. The theme was "Wedding Banquette." It was so simple yet so eloquent. The centerpiece was a large vase of the tallest, most fragrant long-stemmed white roses I have ever seen. I could not take my eyes off them.

I have never been fond of flowers. I do not know why except that maybe flowers are just not a part of my love language. At least not until this very moment. The only thing I could focus on was the flowers and the aroma that filled my nose as I sat there. I could not help but stare at them and try to recollect any time I may have ever received such a beautiful arrangement in my past. Valentine's day? Nope. Anniversaries? Nope. Birthdays? Nope. At my wedding? Nope.

As the night closed, each table sponsor began their clean-up. I hurried around our table to help, and as I was making my way back from the trash, I brushed by the wedding table.

"You did a great job with your table. It is beautiful." I said to the table sponsor.

"Thank you," she replied. "You know, I had planned to give a rose to any lady here God lays on my heart, but I was told to give them all to you. They are not for anyone else but you. I don't know why, but I have a feeling you do." She handed me the vase of roses. My eyes filled with tears. I could not find any words except a quiet "Thank you!"

I held the vase with both hands because the arrangement was huge. I could barely see over the top. Several women passed me, congratulating me as I carried my treasure through the gym.

But as hard as I tried, I could not understand why God would have wanted me to have this vase full of roses. Especially after the hissy fit, I threw earlier in the day. I was embarrassed when I thought about it.

I carried the vase up the stairs to get the kids from the nursery, still thinking, "Why me, God?" Then it hit. Halfway up the stairs. Loud and precise with words so heavy they seemed to hit my stomach like a brick in the water. "See, I do care!"

_____

_____

_____

_____

_____

_____

_____

_____

_____

_____

Father, I thank You that You care about me even when I think You don't see my pain. You see it all and You are close to me.

Psalms 34:18

_____

_____

Cruise Control - Must Be Baby Shampoo

I put my wedding ring in the offering bucket at church one Sunday afternoon. I prayed over it, sealed the envelope, and dropped it in. I still can't say exactly why I filed for divorce, seeing that I prayed so hard for reconciliation except to say that I felt a sense of obligation or responsibility to file. As if I had financial means to file and I didn't, then I was responsible for his living in sin. I know that wasn't entirely true, but it was time to release him to his own will.

I had an attorney who was genuinely kind and honored every request I made. The days, weeks, and months went by very quickly as I awaited the court date. I told my soon-to-be ex-husband he did not have to show up to court. Sign where he needs to sign and return. I did not want him there after all. And he didn't, either. That I was grateful for. I sat by myself on the wooden bench, waiting my turn to go before the judge.

My stomach was queasy, and I thought I would be sick as I waited for what seemed like hours. I found myself praying that this day's events would somehow turn out to be like one of the cheesy chick-flicks where everything turns out to be ok in the end, and they live happily ever after in wedded bliss. But it didn't turn out that way. My attorney made his way in, and we briefly went over what to say and when. I shook my head in acknowledgment of every bit of instruction.

Then finally, it was my turn. I stood as instructed. Answered the appropriate responses, "Yes sir, Your Honor, I am requesting a divorce from my husband on

THINK ABOUT IT...

There is not one place I have traveled He did not go with me. This statement alone is enough to keep me praising the rest of my days.

I did not want a divorce. Walking through those courtroom doors was hard.

Walking out as an officially divorced single mom was even harder.

But I didn't do it alone.

What are the hard things you have walked through that you could sense the presence of God with you as you went through them?

How does knowing He was with you during it all give you comfort?

Is there any situation you need Him to carry you through today?

the grounds of irreconcilable differences." And from there, the gavel pounded down, and the divorce was granted. I walked out of the courtroom and down the hall to the lady's room.

Sitting on the commode, I noted how, up to that moment, not one tear had fallen.

Father, I thank You that I am never left to carry my own burden. In fact, thank You for carrying them for me. I needed You then, I need You now, I need You always. May I feel Your peace through every storm and rest in it. In Jesus name, so be it.

Philippians 4:7

Mind you, I still felt like any minute I could vomit all over the place. But not one single tear had fallen.

The drive home was quiet. I didn't cut on the radio. I rode in silence. Still, not one tear. The kids came home from school. I greeted them as usual, helped them with their homework, cooked supper, and tucked them all in for bed—still, not one single tear. Then the next day, and the next, a week went by. Not one tear graced my cheeks.

It wasn't that I wanted to be a sobbing mess. I didn't. His leaving in the first place hurt more than I could ever put into words. Add to that the insult of being quickly replaced without a second thought. I figured that I would at least have one or two tears left after filing for and going through with divorce proceedings. God knows I did not want this ending.

Sometime later, I was talking to God about that day. About how strange it was. I went through that whole day, the week, with not one single tear. As I dove deep in worship, he showed me why. I saw Him carrying me like a wounded sheep across His shoulders. He said, "I carried you. I sat with you in the courtroom. I carried you up to the front. I held your hand while you talked to the judge. I drove you home. I tucked you in. I carried you." Thank You, Jesus. No more tears.

License Plates - Who's That Girl?

I grew up with the nickname "Kathy," but upon enrollment into the nursing program, I became "Katherine." Katherine is, after all, my birth name. I assume my parents started calling me "Kathy" when our new neighbors moved in. Their daughter, Kathryn, would soon become a part of our Smith clan as she and my sister became best friends. No one in my classes knew me as "Kathy," which was quite refreshing because I did not like her anyway.

Besides, I discovered that one of the greatest benefits of being born again is knowing the old me —Kathy died. She is dead. Hallelujah, the old me is over! The old me was rotten to the core. She was selfish, self-centered, rude, a liar, a pot head, no ambition, and a miserable human being in general. Who in their right mind would want to identify with her? I certainly do not.

So, it comes as no surprise; almost everyone I know (minus my immediate family) knows me and calls me Katherine. It bothers me when someone (not my immediate family) tries to call me "Kathy." It is like nails on a chalkboard. A big no-no in my book, though it may seem silly, or elementary even. When I explain to others why this is, I refer to Abraham or Paul in the Bible. But, let me tell you a story for those who may still have questions or require further illustration.

I was about six or seven years old, visiting my family (aunts, uncles, cousins) at my grandparents' house. My favorite of all my cousins (I will call him Steven) was a year younger than I. The two of us were thick as thieves in those days. He always knew how to make me laugh, and he challenged me often to think outside of the box. This was one of those occasions. The two of us spent most of the day as we usually would, hunting frogs or bugs or whatever disgusting thing we discovered in the great outdoors. Dinner was almost ready, and we were summoned inside to get cleaned up.

My grandparents at the time had a utility room that held a washer and dryer. Off to the side was a modest little bathroom with a toilet, sink, and stand-up shower. I wore a navy-blue dress with ruffles at the bottom, frilly socks with lace on the edges, and black patent-leather sandals. Even in our excursions, I was still fairly clean. He, on the other hand, was not. Somewhere during the handwashing, Steven proposed we change clothes. Not into our own fresh set of clothes, no. He meant to change into each other's clothes, as in SWAP clothes. I vaguely recall us talking about what-ifs. As in what if I were a boy? What if he were a girl?

I stood there in the bathroom, contemplating the idea, and staring at his current wardrobe. He wore an old striped t-shirt and Wrangler boys' jeans. I must have been quite gullible because the next thing I knew, I was standing in the shower wearing his filthy, smelly, dirty, mud-crusted boy clothes. I know those clothes did not stay on my skin more than a minute before I stripped down to his fruit-of-the-loom underwear, demanding my clothes back. There was no way I was going to wear those clothes. It was not part of my DNA to feel comfortable in his clothes.

And there it is this is the reason nobody calls me "Kathy." I no longer share her DNA. I feel as comfortable being referred to as my old self as I did in Steven's dirty clothes. I am not that girl anymore. There is absolutely no part of who I am today that has any desire to relate to or be identified as "Kathy." She is-after-all, dead.

To conclude the narrative, just around the time I opened the shower door to show Steven, who was still wearing my dress, I meant business. The bathroom door opened, and there were both of our parents, grandparents, older siblings, and cousins desperately trying not to laugh.

It is funny how embarrassing stories like this one can serve a greater purpose later in life, isn't it?

_____

_____

_____

_____

_____

_____

_____

_____

_____

_____

Father, I thank You today that all things are made new, and that includes my old nature. Help me to stay centered on You every time I am tempted to identify with someone I am not. I trade my old identity for a new one. As I lean into You, what new name do You have for me? In Jesus name, so be it.

Isaiah 62:2

_____

_____

_____

_____

_____

_____

_____

_____

_____

Backseat Drivers: That's Gotta Suck

"That's gotta suck!" Yes ma'am. That's what I said right before I got a nice little lesson served up during the Christmas season of 2007. "That's gotta suck!" And I can assure you, yes, it does. It was an easy lesson on passing judgment, nicely illustrated by the greatest teacher ever.

The Christmas season has always been packed with excitement for my boys and me, like most families. We decorate our home, and the tree and I wrap each thoughtfully bought gift with love. Every year I try to make each Christmas memorable with their own fingerprint. Meaning, when they are adults, flipping through the pages of Christmas pasts becomes a little easier.

For instance, "That year we all got motor scooters, and mom ate concrete because she had to be the first one to try them out." Or "That year, mom put different names on all of the presents then made us switch at the last minute." Or "When mom wrote the short story about all of us, and we had to figure out who was who." But this one, for me, was marked with its own fingerprint.

I was still in nursing school, nearing my second semester. We had plans to go to my Dad's house for Christmas a few days before, as we usually would. The boys were full of excitement as they all jumped in the back of my four-door Ford Contour. They looked so cute, all bundled up in their coats and knit caps. All three of them sat patiently waiting for me to drive off into the cold December night. I was excited and almost drove halfway there until I realized I forgot to grab a few gifts. I circled back, and all was well.

My dad didn't live far from us, and even though I had to turn around, we would still be a little early. So, I detoured for a few minutes as we drove slowly around nearby

THINK ABOUT IT...

No two persons' journey (or car in this illustration) will look the same.

While I was married, my husband and I had a 1977 Thunderbird, we called "Thunder-Chicken."

It was hideous.

It was tricolor: pink, primer gray and rust. But it served its purpose for a particular season.

I've upgraded several times since then.

Sunroof, blue tooth, backup camera, heated seats-all the bells and whistles.

I found out the hard way not to judge another person's "vehicle."

If you had to describe your "upgrades," what would they look like?

neighborhoods looking at Christmas lights and all the lawn decorations. We admired the candy canes lighting the driveways. Nativity scenes and Snoopy. Giant blow-up Santa and Frosty. And as cheesy as it sounds, the kids were in the back singing Jingle Bells-well-uh, the other Jingle Bells anyway. They would have never been the first to suspect anything was wrong.

After "Oohing and Ahhhing" at the lights and such, I figured it was time to get going. So, I drove along towards my destination. As I attempt to merge onto the main lanes of the Spur, glancing over at my side mirrors as any good driver would, and I get a little peep of smoke in one of my mirrors. I didn't think anything of it. It was December, after all, and quite cold. I continue driving, and pass an exit, then an entrance ramp. Again, I check my mirrors. Yes, I know. I'm such a good driver. I look in the rearview and catch a peek at the kids. They look so cute. And they are not even fighting. Man, I am winning here. My youngest son looked so cute in his floppy cap. I was really having a moment.

One more exit and another entrance ramp. Again, I check my mirrors. There are a lot of cars on the road. It was only about 6ish. The kids were still singing. "Man, that is a lot of smoke. Surely, they know they have a problem." But I didn't stare long. I had an appointment to keep. Eventually, the backseat musical concluded, and we were in an interlude of "who's got more presents." I play along, still trying hard not to be distracted by the dummy driving their jalopy on public streets with smoke pouring out. After all, there were other people on the road.

Finally, my exit neared. With my blinker engaged, I looked over my shoulder for a quick lane change. Here is where I say, "I caught a glimpse of our beautifully wrapped gifts and felt compassion for someone who may not be having a good

Father, I thank You for the redemptive work You have done in me and in others. I ask Your forgiveness for every time I have stood in judgment of a brother or sister on their journey. I understand Your mercy is free for us all. Convict my heart and remind me that my righteousness stinks as dirty rags in Your nostrils when I become an accuser.

Matthew 7:1

day. It was Christmas after all." To my shame, that's not what happened. One more lane change, one more mirror check, and all I can see are headlights and smoke.

"Man, it must suck to be that person right now. It's Christmas, and someone's car just bit the dust." One right turn, a left into the driveway. Yes, Virginia, it does suck to be that person right now.

Merry Christmas. It was me. I suck.

_____

_____

_____

_____

_____

_____

_____

_____

_____

_____

_____

_____

_____

_____

_____

_____

_____

_____

Souvenirs - Good Gifts

"Awe, Dad! We don't like Big Red and Zero Bars! That's not what we asked for!" I smile every time I think about this. And I know it always brings a smile to my sisters and my dad as well. It's an inside joke, but I'll share it in a bit.

Just before I finished nursing school, I decided to do some window shopping for houses. Mind you, I was well-aware of the fact I could do nothing but look. The boys and I were living in a single-wide trailer with my ex-mother-in-law. She shared her home with several dogs and cats as well. In retrospect, all I can say of that time is that God's grace was sufficient for us all. But, as it goes, I knew I would eventually be ready to move out and fly again on my own. It did me good to look around at what could be.

A new subdivision was built across the street from the trailer park I lived in before the divorce called Cary Creek Subdivision. Several homes were built and move-in ready. Curiosity got the better of me; so, the boys and I stopped by for a peek.

It was drizzling outside, and a hard downpour threatened the skies. We drove in towards the back for the "Open House" tour. The boys and I walked the home, through every room, exploring closets and such. Once we were done, the office manager thanked us for stopping by. I had to ask, "How much are these homes going for?" He responded, "175,000." And with that, I politely thanked the gentleman for his time, and we ran out to our car. I remember thinking, "God, I'd like a house like this one day. You can do that, right?" And that was the end of my window shopping.

Fast forward another two years. I graduated from nursing school and landed a good job. Correction landed the

THINK ABOUT IT...

Before I moved into my new house, I was starting to think I would never own my own home.

Before then, I thought I would never finish the nursing program and get a good job.

Before then, I was so worried my boys and I would be out on the streets.

My point is that every single time I have been in need, He supplied. And He did so in grandeur. I am in awe of His provision.

Do you need provision in any area of your life?

How has God shown You the grandeur of His provision?

perfect job for me at the time. I faithfully saved my money in preparation for buying my kids and me a new home. I looked at several houses and had a realtor friend help me along the way.

I found a lovely home that I really liked. It had vaulted ceilings, a fireplace, big rooms, and a nice kitchen. I told God, "I want this one." It was a foreclosure home, so the price was reasonable. I had my realtor friend put in a bid for me. The seller and I went back and forth on the agreements, but he found another buyer before anything could be settled, and the house was sold.

A few weeks later, I looked at another home I really liked, even better than the first one. It was in a nice neighborhood, two-story, granite countertops, and stainless-steel appliances. I told God, "I want this one." I prayed. I decreed. I declared. I did the Jericho march all around that house. It was mine. I put in my bid, played ping-pong

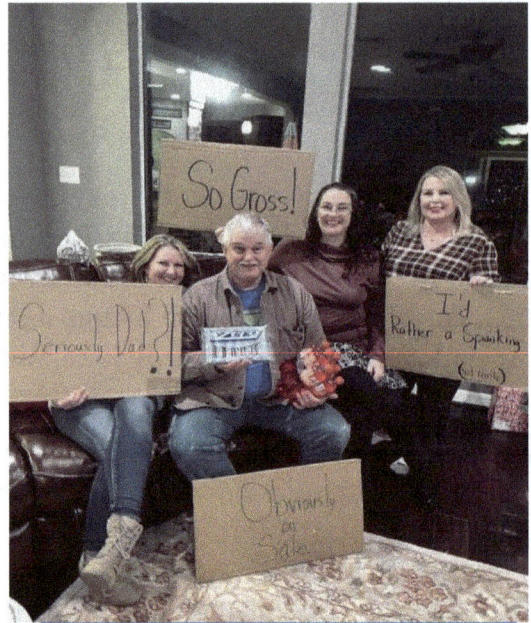

Photo taken Christmas 2020 with my Dad and sisters. We surprised him with Big Red and Zero Bars!

again with the seller. I remember at one point hearing distinctively Holy Spirit whisper, "Do you trust Me?" I quickly responded, "I do." "Do you trust Me?" I heard again. "You know I do, Father," I replied. But, yet again, the home was swept right out from underneath me—more disappointment.

Finally, I said to God, "Ok, I'm not getting my hopes up again. You find me a house. I don't want to get excited if I don't know for sure it's the one You have for me." Amen?

So, now let me tell you about those Zero bars. My grandparents live in Livingston, TX, about an hour and a half from where I lived growing up. When my parents would drive out there, we would stop at this little country store on the way. It looked like a little country store, complete with outhouses in the back. Anyway, like most kids, we all had small bladders, so mom and dad would stop at this store to let us all go potty while they bought us girls a drink. (There are four of us sisters.)

On one of our trips out to Grandma's house, we stop at this store. Dad asks us all what drink and candy we want. "Dr Pepper and a Snickers." "Coke and Snickers." "Sunkist and 3 Musketeer bar." "Sprite and a bag of Skittles." Surely dad was paying attention as he went inside with his mental list. But he didn't. He came back to the van with a bag full of Big Red Sodas and Zero Bars. None of which any of us sisters wanted.

While we were almost crying in disappointment, Dad thought it was hilarious. And he was quite satisfied with his purchase because he loves Big Red and Zero bars! None of us girls found it funny until we were grown. Now, it is one of our favorite memories. No surprise, I had trust issues!

So, several weeks go by after the last house deal fell through. I was scrolling through the real estate listings out of boredom when I stumbled across a cute little house on Cary Creek. Foreclosure. Three-bedroom, two-bath, nice sized kitchen, two-car garage, and office space. Nice, I thought. Maybe I will stop by. I got in my car and drove over there to have a look. Standing in the yard, looking up the street, I could not figure out which house it was I looked at two years

Father, I thank You that You are my provider and that You know what You are doing. I understand that You know what I have need of before I ever even knew I needed it. I receive Your provision right now. In Jesus name, so be it.

Matthew 7:11

before. Several more homes were built on that street since then, and most of them resembled each other. They were cookie-cutter homes with three different styles. I called my real estate friend and had her look into it. She called me the next day. "Have you seen the inside of this home? You have got to go look at it." I told her no, I hadn't because the door had a lockbox on the doorknob. "Go look at it. I'll give you the code. It's easy—A-M-E-N."

"Tell me you did that, Myra. No way," I responded. "No, that's the code. This is it." I went by the house after work for a walk-through. The house was in remarkable shape and still looked brand new. We put in a bid that same afternoon. No surprise, I bought the house at a very reasonable price, and in no time, the boys and I moved in. We moved into our new three-bedroom brick home right across the street from the mobile home park God delivered me from almost four years to the date. Talk about from the pit to the palace! About two weeks later, the neighbor stops by with a plate of cookies to welcome us to the neighborhood. We chatted for a bit about the home, the neighborhood, schools, etc.

Finally, she said, "You know, this used to be the Open House, right? When they were just building the neighborhood, this house was the Showcase House." And just like that, I was taken back to that moment, just a few years before. "God, I'd like a house like this one day. You can do that, right?"

He didn't show up with a Big Red and Zero Bar, did He?

_____

_____

_____

_____

_____

_____

_____

_____

_____

_____

_____

_____

_____

Back-up Camera – Yes, I was pouting...

February 14, 2010

"I'm done believing in anything." The kids came home from their dad's wedding. They were dressed so cute in their black suits. I would have been a proud momma wanting to take a picture of the three of them and show it off to everyone I know if it didn't bring back so many awful memories of this day only five years before. To say I was disappointed would be an understatement.

Below is an excerpt from a journal entry:

April 4, 2005

"Father, I come to You in the name of Jesus. Help me through this time. Even as I write, Father, I feel so lost. Almost as though I misread things. Is it over? For Good? For now? My heart hurts so bad. I know why I withdrew last night. I know I am holding on to the past. When I think back to those younger days, was I stupid? I wished I'd known what I know now.

No wonder things didn't work out. I've not only done myself wrong, (him) wrong, but I hurt my kids. I am so ashamed of myself. I think that is why I am having such a hard time accepting that it's over. I don't want to be the person in ministry teaching women that healing marriage may not be possible. It makes me think of our children as adults telling others our parents just couldn't get it together.

Father Your word says that whosoever delights in You, You shall grant their hearts desires. Father, he doesn't hate me. I don't hate him. Father, I don't want this testimony.

Father, I ask that You heal my heart completely of disappointment and forgive me for allowing that disappointment to become a barrier or stumbling block in my walk with You. I receive Your forgiveness and healing in Jesus' name, so be it.

Hebrews 4:14-16

Father, I know You have done great work for other women, but I REALLY DON'T WANT THIS TESTIMONY. I still want to give other women hope. I want to give my kids the testimony my parents could not provide me of Your (marital) reconciliation, and our kids will have a front-row seat."

My begging went on for more than just a few pages. It went on for five years. Right up until the day those wedding bells rang and the fact they weren't mine brought a new kind of mourning I never knew.

So, when it didn't go the way I begged God to do things, I did the only thing I knew how to do for that season—I pouted. I say that humorously though it was not funny.

I wish I had a backup camera.

_____

_____

_____

_____

_____

_____

_____

_____

_____

_____

_____

_____

Taking Calls – Sorry, Wrong Number

Have you ever put yourself in a position you knew very well going into that you had no business getting into? No, of course, you haven't. Only I would do that. When I reflect on some of the things I've done after giving my heart to God, I cannot help but thank Him for His tender mercies that are brand new every day. If you haven't discovered yet, I have done some pretty silly things. Beyond silly. Stupid. (Oh-my-gosh-this-is-so-embarrassing-but-I'm-gonna-share-it-anyway!) Ok, here goes.

"Being single sucks. Yes, Jesus and I are tight, and He's my best friend. But being single sucks. "This was my mindset several years ago. I am thankful my children were young at the time. So, naturally, like any single and looking gal would, I signed up on a dating website.

I made myself look good! My dating profile was on point! I made sure to let all prospects know I love Jesus with all of my heart.

My bait was on the hook, I cast the line, and now I'm reeling them in.

No, not every fish made the cut. All but one was catch and release. This one was a keeper; after all, he understood

THINK ABOUT IT...

Loneliness is something I struggled with horribly for so long. I spent more than half of my life in some sort of relationship, and I did not know how to enjoy life as a single woman. I went around this mountain a few times before I got the message.

I tried to find my friend recently on social media. I guess I was just being nosy, but it turns out God saved my life yet again.

Turned out, my friend returned to some very dangerous addictions and beat up his girlfriend severely. He was shot and killed when he returned to her house to finish what he started.

Is there anything scripted into your journey You know wasn't authored by Him?

Are there situations you have scripted that He, in His mercy, warned and protected you from?

my reference to Boaz.

We talked every day. He had a great personality. We got along wonderfully. We talked about Jesus and all the marvelous things He's done for us. He prayed for me. I prayed for him. I met his mom. He met my ex-mother-in-law. (I wish you could hear the humor in my tone-though this is TOTALLY and 100% true.)

He was a nice guy and all, recently released from prison and a recovering alcoholic missing his front teeth from a barroom brawl. I found a gem. (All humor aside, he was born again and trying to start a new life. Jesus loves him, too.)

One afternoon when the house was empty, he came over to visit. He wasn't Prince Charming, but he wasn't an ugly toad either. I truly enjoyed his company,

Father, I thank You for Your protection over me. I ask that You give me wisdom and discernment with every decision I make. I thank You that You know every situation from beginning to end and have only my best interest at heart. In Jesus name, so be it.

Hebrews 12:2

and I valued him as a friend. Up to this point, and even after, I cannot say I was physically attracted to him. But, like I said, "Being single sucks," and obviously, this area in my life was one I hadn't dealt with until this one afternoon anyway.

It's hard to say precisely what happened or how mainly because it's so embarrassing. I can admit lines were crossed, and it was totally selfish on my part. (Pay attention ladies, ownership is important.) I will leave out all of the dirty details because THANK YOU, Jesus, for barging into my room and tapping me on the shoulder and speaking in a voice I could not ignore BEFORE anything happened that I could not take back. THANK YOU! THANK YOU! THANK YOU!

"A-hem…what are you doing? What Are You Doing? I DID NOT PUT HIM IN YOUR LIFE. YOU DID. WHAT ARE YOU DOING?" Well, the curtains fell, and the show was over. I retreated in tears and showed him the door.

"Okie Dokie! That's all You had to say, Jesus. Yes sir! I hear You! I'm so sorry, bud. You gotta go. Wrong number."

_____

_____

_____

_____

_____

_____

_____

_____

_____

_____

_____

_____

_____

_____

_____

_____

_____

_____

Bluetooth – Hands Free Please

I am a slow learner. At least in this area, I am. "Being single sucks." There it is again. A few years later, one more trip around the mountain. But at least this time, my fish was tall, handsome, not an ex-convict, had all his teeth, smelled great, and a pastor's son. Winner-winner-chicken-dinner! And this time, I had the added benefit of knowing my worth and value and stood firm on my convictions that my body is a temple. Before I go any further, let's talk about my history with this particular subject. Yes, more dirt and embarrassing secrets.

Like many other gals I know, the devil attacked me at an early age with rejection. It is not uncommon and is an undeniably effective tool in Satan's toolbox. And it wreaked havoc in my life at the tender age of 13. I equated early in life sex for love and acceptance, from males and females alike. I wasted most of my teen and young adult years chasing hard after love and acceptance. The sad truth is there was not much of me left by the time I came to Jesus. Thankfully, by the time I met this fella, I understood the spiritual principles associated with sex and had no desire to give myself away nor prostitute the blood of Jesus in my life. Heavy words, I know. Thankfully, I carried this strong conviction in my heart. But this gal still had a thing or two to learn about fishing.

He smelled good. He was tall and robust, with a deep voice to match a smooth tongue. On our first date, we met for dinner at a nice restaurant. We went to a movie. We sat in his car after and talked for what seemed like hours. He took an interest in me, in my life, in my children. He laughed at my jokes, told me I was beautiful, and apologized for every man who ever hurt me. And he smelled good. Yes, I know. I mentioned that already.

Father, I ask You to seal in my heart my worth and value to You. I understand I am irreplaceable. Father help me to let go completely of loneliness and disappointment. Return every piece of me I have given away to others who were underserving. Cause 100% of my heart and affection be towards You to allow Your perfect will in my life. In Jesus name, so be it.

Psalm 119:36-37

On our second date, he picked me up, and we went to the downtown Aquarium. We ate dinner. He took me on a carriage ride. It was almost Christmas; the streets lit with lights. We cuddled together in the carriage, shared our first kiss and our second and third. He seemed to have grown an extra set of hands, though–but he smelled good.

On our third "date," he came over to the house after the kids were in bed. I made it clear I was not ready for my boys to meet him until I knew the relationship was going somewhere. He said he understood. It was also understood, or so I thought, that if he were looking for someone to hook up with or "try on," I was not that woman. We stood by his SUV with his trunk open as we talked, cuddled, kissed, and made out. Soon those extra sets of arms sprouted. And even though he smelled good, this gal had her convictions. I was getting a little irritated. The lure of his cologne wore off, and now there is an elephant in my yard.

A few nights go by, and I did not hear from him. When I did, he made it clear he wanted more. I made it clear that his two arms were two too many. I can't say it didn't hurt. It did. I remember crying out to God in prayer, "God, why does this hurt so bad? I am not 13 anymore."

Next time, Jesus, You dial. Bluetooth all the way.

Making a Right Turn

I sat there at the intersection, gripping tightly to my steering wheel, fretting about which turn to make. I looked at my boys strapped in the car, who were 14, 11, and 9 at the time. They were looking at me with anticipation, waiting on me to choose which turn I would make—Left? Right? While their little hearts were set on which way I should turn, I had a decision to make. (There's that word again-" decision.")

My spirit was awakened by the disappointment I felt in my "Bluetooth" experience. Were there not any men of God anymore who stood firm on the word of God? There in my car were three up-and-coming young men I knew needed to be raised knowing how to be that man.

I also had a righteous anger building inside to follow the plan of God for my life with my whole heart.

I wanted that plan more than I wanted to be "felt up." In short, I wanted to step into the call of God on my life. I knew, with no hesitation, there were major decisions to be made.

Make a left turn, and I choose familiarity. Make a right turn, and I choose faith in the unknown. I sat at this stop sign for what seemed like hours. My knuckles were turning white from gripping the steering wheel so hard. I don't remember if there was anyone behind me or waiting on me to turn. It didn't matter to me anyway. My boys were voicing their

THINK ABOUT IT...

I wanted the will, plan and purpose God had for me more than anything.

I was torn between familiarity and stepping into the unknown.

I had my fill of trying to force it to happen my way, which ended up with four left turns.

Yep, I ran in circles trying to force the hand of God to do things my way.

So why not take that leap of faith, make that right turn and let Him take the wheel from here?

desires. The oldest had tears running down his face. I did not want to disappoint him or either one of them.

"Boys, listen to your momma. I know God has great plans for my life, and I want it all. I must follow Him. I must give it a shot. You don't know what God has for you there, but it will be good. Please believe in your momma."

I made a right turn. Finally, a right turn. And it was a good one. I pulled into the "Celebration of Life Church" parking lot with my three young men.

I remember the first sermon I heard that morning about stepping into and processing the call of God on your life. No more confirmation is needed for me. I began to volunteer shortly after with the youth ministry. A few weeks in, the youth pastor wrote prophetic words on construction paper for each youth—one word. I approached him to ask for one for me. Guess what word that was – royalty!

Father, forgive me ever trying to force my will upon You. I understand the importance of surrendering my will to Yours. Show me where the right turn is. You lead me and I will follow. In Jesus name, so be it.

Isaiah 30:21

_____

_____

_____

_____

_____

_____

Driving in the Dark - Cover Me

It was 3:30 in the morning, and my alarm wasn't set to wake until 5:30. My busy nursing shift was just a few hours away, and little did I know I would be clocking in looking like one hot mess of a woman.

Yep. 3:30 in the am. I can't say I woke up because I was dreaming. I wasn't. Or that I was startled by a strange noise. My eyes simply popped open for no good reason at all. Those who know me well can testify that I can and have slept through a hurricane.

I've been in the habit for several years of offering a "Good Morning Holy Spirit" hand wave as soon as I awake. I waved my hand but quickly decided after checking the time that it was too early to be awake. I rolled over and got comfortable again, but I was still awake. I closed my eyes, but I was awake.

I've heard many testimonies of how Holy Spirit chooses some rather inopportune times to have a conversation with us. It does make sense (at least for me anyway) because my mind seems to run a mile a minute during my waking hours-that Holy Spirit would choose to strike up a conversation in the wee early morning hours with a gentle tap and a polite "A-hem." But (and that's important), BUT I have the choice to respond or send Him to voicemail. I chose to respond.

To understand the conversation that would change everything for me, let me lay down some framework. At the time, I'd been saved around seven years. I gave my life to Jesus face down on my living room carpet, February 14, 2005, after it was apparent my marriage was officially over. My husband came in from work that evening and handed me a card that read, "Thanks for all the years." From there,

THINK ABOUT IT...

Being hungry is never pleasant until that hunger is satisfied.

I love witnessing to people with this one snippet of my life.

I wanted understanding of why I was hurting so bad. At times I felt like a toddler with an ailment, but no way to express what was wrong.

Looking at what was hidden deep within was not pleasant, but the love He poured out for me has forever changed my heart. It was a pure expression of love I chase after to this day.

Nothing else satisfies. Nothing!

Have you ever had a 3:30am awakening to His love?

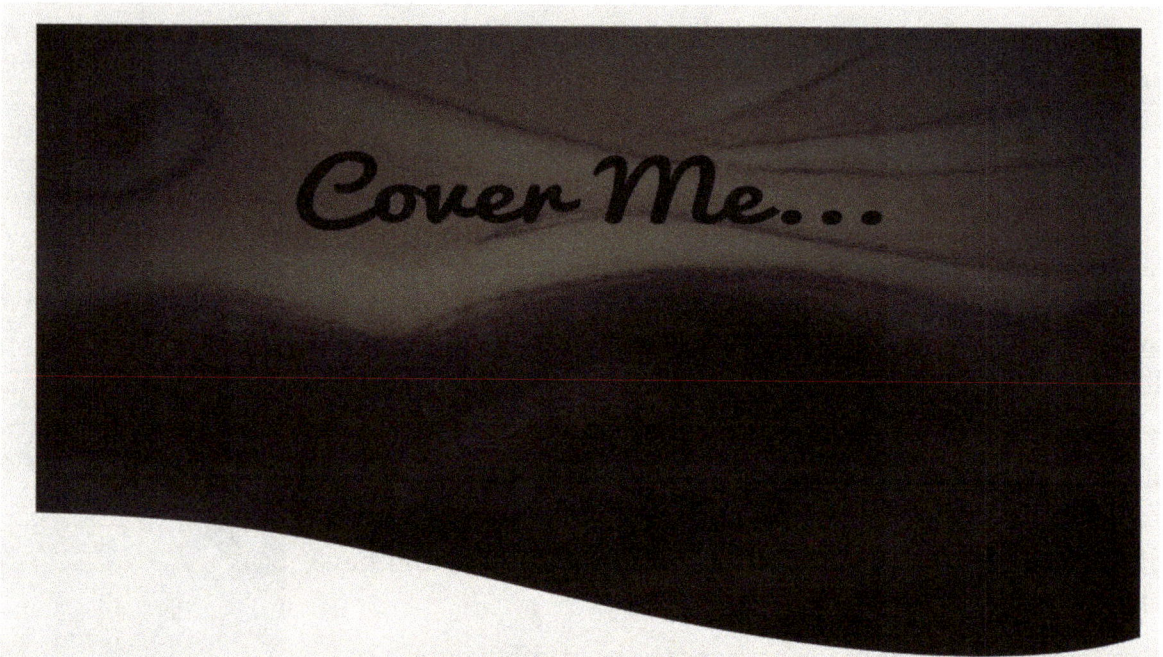

Cover Me...

he promptly showered, shaved, and got dressed for a first date with who would later be his second wife.

To say I was devastated would be an understatement, but that's a whole other narrative for a later time. Right then, I finally fell forward in submission and surrendered to Jesus. I phrase my born-again experience like that because it's the truth. Several times throughout my life, I attempted to live for Him, but surrender was not a concept I could grasp-and quite honestly, I don't think I would have surrendered anyway until that particular day.

While up to this point of salvation, I never experienced an intimate relationship with Jesus or the Word of God. My small bank of knowledge held the Salvation Prayer and basic theoretical principles of faith. Things like healing, restoration, and the power of prayer. I soon committed myself to a church, and a relationship with Jesus started to develop.

Original charcoal drawing by K. Renteria created to express the tangible likeness of the blanket of Love and Peace I felt during this encounter with Holy Spirt.

Over the next several years, I continued to grow and flourish. I read the Bible, studied, prayed, and soaked up as much of His presence as I could. Oftentimes, I would find myself in awe of His goodness towards my children and me. I was baptized and received my prayer language. Healing began to come to areas of my life from my childhood as I began to see a small glimpse of the plan of God for my life. It was in the early months that I received the call into ministry.

I stood in faith the entire time for my marriage to be restored. I prayed repeatedly and agreed with others in prayer that God would touch his heart to come home. I prayed right up to the day the two of them were married some years later, on February 14th. I encountered an array of emotions—anger, bitterness, confusion, embarrassment, and loneliness. In short, if my emotions were an amusement park, there would be no shortage of rollercoaster rides, and the refreshments would be stale, and way overpriced.

Towards the end of this period, I came to believe God had just about enough of my hissy fits. I am a parent, and I can totally relate! I began to feel that tug on my heart, and I still found myself with a pure desire to see the plan of God for my life unfold. "BUT!" This is a big word for three little letters. But, as I attempted to climb my way out of the pit I was in, I hit a massive brick wall.

"I can't hear You!" "I can't feel You!" "Please don't take Your hands off of me!" These were things I constantly found myself praying for. At 3:30 in the morning, God, in His merciful and tender way, made His way into my bedroom to speak to me and finally tear down the wall I unknowingly built around my heart.

I've had a queen-sized to myself for a while now, and the only thing I've had to snuggle with was my pillow and blankets. And obviously, the room was pitch black, and the only noise was coming from the box fan on full blast by my bed. After maybe a minute or two lying there, I was acutely aware I was not alone. I was reminded of Samuel's response when he heard Him call in the middle of the night. So, I softly whispered in my sleepy whisper, "I'm here, Father. What do You want to say to me?"

Several minutes seemed to pass as I waited. My thoughts started turning to work and nursing things when suddenly I felt a blanket of peace come over me. I mean, a tangible-feeling blanket of peace swept over me physical body—starting at my feet, over my legs, back, and arms. I began to feel warm and completely relaxed. It was an undeniable and incredible feeling. Soon tears began to flow uncontrollably, one after another as a profound expression of pure love now accompanied this peace blanket. I felt more acceptance, tenderness, and intimacy right then than I had ever felt in my whole life. I knew right then that this was what I'd been chasing after since I was a young girl.

All I could perceive was, "I love you, Katherine. I love you. I love you. I love you." I was "cuddling" with the Love of God and wept as He began to speak.

(I find it challenging to accurately describe a "God-chat" as there is no audible dialogue to be recorded and replayed. He speaks to me through images/pictures in my mind, impressions, and a soft inner voice. It's left to my interpretation and confirmed with peace and an inner-knowing affirmation.)

A quick mental video played in my mind. It was a question I thought I deserved to know the answer to.

Pondering in recollection of my state of mind back then, I can't help but chuckle a little at the fact that I believed I was entitled to an answer to any question I may have had. It is pretty funny to me now after the response I was given, and I agree that this is one of those embarrassing stories some parents might tell about their children when they are grown.

"Why on Valentine's Day? Why did it have to be on Valentine's Day? Of all days. Why on a day universally recognized as a day for love and acceptance?" Upon hearing myself ask this question, I could feel the anguish I felt the day he left begin to emerge.

But His response would provoke even deeper anguish.

"You don't know, Love." He whispered softly to my spirit as He gently began to explain.

"You made him your idol." He was showing me my heart, and it was not something I could be proud of. "You made him your idol." I wish I could describe the imagery here. I made my ex an idol! I felt two inches tall. Really. I curled my legs up to a fetal position and wept from utter repentance. I felt as if I would throw up at any moment. "You made him your idol."

Gross. I made an idol out of a man who packed his bags and walked out on our three children and me. Who left me a heaping hot mess to fend for myself? I made THAT my idol?!?! I laid there in my bed and wept out loud. Verbally repenting. Begging for forgiveness. "I love You so much. I love You so much, Father. I didn't know. I love You so much." I remember this to be my exact response. I repeated it over and over with recollection after recollection of His goodness towards me.

"I love You so much. I love You so much, Father. I didn't know. I love You so much." As I cried out to Him, there He was. He was holding me closer to Him with forgiveness and acceptance, oozing out all over me. I can almost hear the consolation in His embrace like a momma does her crying infant. There was no condemnation present at that moment. I was feeling nauseous-He was only feeling pure LOVE for me.

HE is TRUE LOVE! I get it! I finally get it! I thought I understood before this early morning chat. The truth is, I hadn't begun to experience the fulness of the healing He wanted to bring me. I surrendered to Him once again, and He began to peel back all the band-aids I placed on the hurt. Not only the wounds of betrayal and a failed marriage but dozens of others I kept buried like ugly secrets. In the months ahead, each would be exposed, confronted, reconciled, and healed.

To date, I still have my challenges. And I am sure there will always be things He and I need to chat about, but I can't think of any other time I have been as thankful as I am today for being awakened at 3:30 in the morning.

_____

_____

Father, I thank You that You are the purest expression of love that exists because You are love. There is no part of You that knows any other ways. I thank for Your patience, kindness, goodness, and mercy that chases me down until the early hours of the morning to pour out Your love over me. In Jesus name, so be it.

1 Corinthians 13:4-7

_____

_____

_____

_____

Visor Mirrors: Borrowed Jeans

"Wow! Look at her go. She's so anointed. She's got doors opening up left and right. Why can't I have a testimony like hers? I wish I had her testimony." These are thoughts I once held towards a few close friends of mine many years ago. That is until I was sharply redirected back into my own lane. "Don't despise your testimony nor judge yourself amongst others. I can't use what you don't own."

Welcome, to this week's episode of "This Girl has Problems." Grab your popcorn and cold beverage (ha-ha). I have been born again for a little more than 15 years now. God healed me of a broken heart, delivered me from a spirit of rejection and drug abuse.

I went from basically being uneducated and penniless to owning my own home and having a promising career in healthcare. Plus, my relationship with my dad has been mended and strengthened.

Original sketch "Borrowed Jeans" K Renteria

God has done several amazing things for me. He forgave me of my sins, adopted me into His Kingdom, and I'm on my way to Heaven. What is there not to appreciate?

But still, without fail, I would find my self-entertaining "testimony jealousy."

As if my testimony was worthless and void of power to help someone else. I am so thankful for the correction from Holy Spirit. I understood, immediately,

I don't know about you, but jealousy does not look good on me. I received a sharp re-direct on this subject.

Yes, I can be in awe of what God has done in someone else's life and ask Him to do the same for me, but it is never ok to despise my own history with God.

What I failed to consider, with this whole line of thinking, "Her testimony is greater than mine," is actually saying "Jesus, what You did for me in my life was not good enough."

When I stop and take inventory of what He has done for me, I am in awe!

How could I ever try to slash the price Jesus paid for me?

Have you ever wished you could wear someone else's testimony instead of your own?

the assault I placed on the blood of Jesus Christ in my own life by comparing myself with others. As if what He did for me was not enough. Silly woman.

I tried on my middle son's (who is tall and slender) blue jeans one day to see if they fit. Yes, I did. A forty-four-year-old, 150ish pound woman tried on his Abercrombie ripped, stone-washed slim, relaxed-fit jeans. They were a bit baggy on him but looked nice on me. I've lost quite a bit of weight over the last year. I've gotten to wear things now I would never dare before. I was curious, so I put them on. I pulled them up over my thighs, around my waist, and zipped them up. No problem. No muffin top either, which was a bonus. I did not say I can rock those jeans. I cannot wear them like he does because they are not made for my build. They were made for him. Even more importantly, they were not mine. He had been wearing them for so long; they were conformed to his build and stature.

I can speak about many things. But while borrowed jeans are convenient, I can't offer them to anyone else cause I have no ownership. No history. No authority. And, what's more, nobody in their right mind buys a pair of shoes to go with borrowed jeans.

Father, I ask that You reveal to me any time I have thought or believed that what You have done for me is in any way unimportant or unusable in Your kingdom. I understand that You use everything for Your glory and that nobody else's testimony can replace the power in my own. In Jesus name, so be it.

2 Corinthians 10:12

_____

_____

_____

_____

_____

New Brakes-One More Momma

I sat across from a spiritual giant in my eyes. A woman I admired from afar. The woman who bear-hugged me the first time I stepped foot into Celebration of Life Church and whispered in my ear, "Welcome Home." A woman who whispered those exact words into my heart some years later after I lost sight of who I was. Momma Linda, who I would learn to call her, sat across from me at the table in anticipation of our conversation.

"I am so glad to be here with you today, enjoying our time together," she started.

"You asked me the other day if I would be your mentor.

I just wanted to sit down with you and honor you and your request.

And know a little bit more about how I can serve you. How can I serve the God in you?

What are your expectations in your request?" I probably looked like a deer in headlights. I was in fearful awe. I knew in my spirit this was a marked moment with the thumbprint of Jesus all over it. I was sitting at the table with Momma Linda Walker, a lady I (and all of us in God's Kingdom) know the devil runs when she wakes up in the morning.

THINK ABOUT IT...

I always tell people there are a few key things I learned that are crucial in spiritual development.

After being born again, we must be in an environment conducive to Holy Spirit, baptized by the Holy Spirit, have a healthy daily intake of prayer, worship and the Word of God, and people we trust Him enough to correct us when we are out of line and to speak into our lives.

It takes a lot of trust and honor on both parts. I love my "Mommas" as I call them. They teach, lead, and correct with the same love and tenderness as a momma. They also defend like a momma cat does her babies.

Do you have someone you trust to be your "momma" mentor?

If you have mentors, what have you been able to glean from them?

Wisdom, love, and patience ooze from her being—it's a part of her. I love to watch her minister to others. She does so with the tenderness of a momma's heart but the tenacity and ferocity of a general. I want to be like her when I grow up.

"Well," I proceeded, "I feel like I am in a transitional period in my life, and I need guidance. I don't want pats on the back, but wisdom, impartation, correction—all of it." Hey, I'm not even going to lie; that "correction" request came with much trembling. But I knew I needed it in my life. And she was the woman for the job.

I've learned to lean into Momma Linda's "chit-chat's" and to glean from all God has given her to pour out. She has taught me so much over the last several years—how to love well, serve well, forgive well, shut up and listen, and how to kick the

Father, I thank You that in Your wisdom and mercy, You have placed people in my life that You knew I would need to be fruitful in my walk with You. I pray blessings over each of these people. Father, I ask You to show me who You would have me reciprocate that role to and lead and teach me as I say "yes." In Jesus name, so be it.

John 15:16

devil in the teeth. I've watched her minister in a Cracker Barrell, the church doors, at the altar, and on the mission fields both home and abroad. I've listened as she preached from the pulpit; and taken notes from the messages of her life.

I needed another Momma. Nobody needs just one.

(Momma Linda-I honor you and the force-to-be-reckoned-with-God in you. I am honored to be a spiritual daughter of yours. Thank you for your prayers, kindness, correction, wisdom, love, and support. I love you more.)

Roadside Assistance: Dog Tired

My loving, generously giving ex-mother-in-law gave the kids and me a crack-puppy for a housewarming present. Ok, so that's not entirely true. There was no bow. (I do still need to send a thank-you note, though). But she certainly did bring us a crack puppy. He was a four-legged Adderall poster pup if there ever was one. 13 pounds of pure spunk with long, silky grey hair and a curved tail. What breed, you ask? It doesn't matter. His name by his previous owner was Sparky. Fitting, but not 100%. Within the first twenty hours in our home-we re-named him, Doofus.

Which was a more "spiritually correct" name for another term more commonly used by society, but I didn't want my kids using that kind of language. His first night with us was a sleepless one. His favorite game, we soon discovered, was fetch (like most pups). The kids played with him all day. Back and forth over and over. You'd think he would have been tired by the end of the day. Nope. Though the house was dark and quiet, and we had a usual 6:00 am alarm set for the next day, this little guy had his own schedule to keep. Oh yeah, did I mention he came with a cute little collar with bells? Or that the main part of our house has a tiled floor?)

We could hear him running all through the house for what seemed like hours. He went back and forth through my room, the living room, the dining room, and back to my room. Over and over and over again with his little belled collar and his nails scurrying across the floor. Needless to say, I invested in a kennel the next day. Smart move on my part.

Our pup had an adorable little trot as well. It's as if one of his legs were shorter than the others or his hind legs moved faster than his front legs. Either way, he'd get

THINK ABOUT IT...

I love my fur babies. Admittedly, I am not a "dog person," but I have bonded well with Doofus. We have an understanding. I have another fur baby named Marley.

He is a mini-Schnauzer and twenty-five pounds of pure stubbornness.

I could say our personalities clash, but I would be lying. We are probably made for each other. I tell him to go to bed, he lays down right at my feet and rolls over, then will not move.

I had that same stubbornness. Thankfully, it's been loved right out of me. He still choses to pick me up, snuggle with me, correct, feed, and bath me.

When has He chosen to pick you up and carry you despite your character flaws?

What has He "loved right out of you?"

excited and trip himself up. Sometimes he'd have trouble coming to a controlled halt and end up running into the sofa or the door if he needed to go out. It was pretty adorable but seemed to make his name that much more fitting.

One afternoon, I was getting myself ready for a walk. I had my tennis shoes on. I grabbed my water, and Doofus was begging me with his puppy face to go. I leashed him up with the harness, and off we went.

My usual route is three miles and lacks shade. The leash I had was one of those retractable leashes that allows flexible distances so that I could give him plenty of room. I enjoyed my walks around the neighborhood. It's quiet time where I'm forced to be quiet and listen. Otherwise, I'd be known as "that crazy lady who talks to herself."

We were about 3/4 in when I noticed he was getting tired. I guess his little crazy legs were finally exhausted. I gave him a few minutes to collect himself and rest as I gave him some water. Keep in mind; it's late May. I live in Texas, and patience was not a fruit of the Spirit I walked in on this evening. Even when the sun goes down, it's hot, and my right guard had taken a left turn about a mile back (yes, I was starting to stink). After a few minutes, we went on, but not for long. He was worn out. He parked his cute little furry behind right in the middle of the street and would not budge.

I stared my little furry friend down with both annoyance and sympathy because this turned out to be a bad idea. I was going to have to carry him the rest of the way.

To make matters worse, my poor little Doofus was in desperate need of a bath. If anything smelled worse than me right then, it was my dog.

I picked him up in my arms and kept walking. He was so thankful he offered his wet, slobbery, dog-breath kisses all over my face. It wasn't too long before he flopped himself on his back and relaxed in my arms as I carried him. Even though I was aggravated, I praised and loved on him while I walked. Once we got closer to my house, I told myself, "Remember this next time," to serve as a reminder of the consequence of taking him along on my walks.

But just as I sat him down in the grass, I heard a different reminder. "I don't mind it when I have to carry you, Katherine." As silly as it seems, such could serve as a lesson for us all. He carries us when we are exhausted. He carries us when we stink (from our self-made messes). He carries us and even chooses to love on us while He does.

_____

_____

_____

_____

_____

_____

Father, I thank You that You love me just as I am, and You love me too much to leave as I am. I ask that You show me how I can partner with You and lay my head on Your shoulder at the same time. In Jesus name, so be it.

Song of Solomon 6:3

_____

_____

_____

_____

_____

"I Spy" - Hide and Sweep

The boys and I got busy on a Saturday afternoon, as usual, to do housework. I know, I know, not a fun way to spend an afternoon, but hey, it's not going to clean itself. And, like most kids, we went through our usual routine of "But why?" "Because I said so" and "Do you call that clean?" routine. (Mom, I am so sorry if I ever gave you any trouble when it came to cleaning.)

I did most of the scrub work while the boys cleaned their rooms, folded laundry, and took out the trash. For the most part, the boys stayed on task as we listened to some of my favorite old country music.

When I first bought our home, one of the things I liked about it was the flooring. The large, open entryway leads directly into our living and dining room. It looks and feels very spacious, even with all the furniture. After living there for a few months, I soon discovered just how fast and dirty even a dark faux wood floor can become. Sweeping becomes quite tiresome when going after that "spotless" clean.

This one afternoon of cleaning was no different. I was wearing myself out, trying to get the floor to shine. It appears every time I left the room for something, another gust of dirt wind would blow right through the house again. I was tired, sweaty, and ready to be finished already.

Around mid-afternoon, the sun shines directly on the front of the house. It is lovely in many ways. So here I am, sweeping the floor for the umpteenth time. I was cranky by then. Gabriel, who was about six, I think at the time, walks through the living room, looks at me, sweeping, and opens the front door.

THINK ABOUT IT...

It is amazing how much dirt you can see in dark spaces when the light shines in.

I have experienced this in many areas of my life.

What has been illuminated in your life during your journey?

Can you remember times in your life when you needed some housework done and the love light of Jesus reveal the dirt in your life?

"There you go, mom. It's just like when we let Jesus in. The light comes in and shows us where all the dirt is hiding." He said as he turned and left the room, and suddenly, whuala. I could see all the dirt and dust I was missing in all those nooks and crannies–sweeping made easy.

I just stood there frozen for a second, holding on to my broom, dumbfounded. In shock that (1) I hadn't thought of that first and (2) that my youngest child, who barely learned how to read, had that kind of revelation.

Yeah! While doing housework, I found that my children are paying attention, and there is an easier way to get my floor clean faster.

_____

_____

_____

_____

_____

_____

_____

_____

_____

_____

Exploring the Dashboard – Look at all the Pretty Colors

I have always had a flare for art and writing. As a young girl, I could draw and paint well, and this gift was not as developed as it is today. I have always enjoyed creating something uniquely mine. Not for the intent for public display necessarily, but for me. "I did that." It has given me a sense of great accomplishment and pride.

As a young teenager, Grandpa would encourage me in this gift. "You could make lots of money with your artwork. It just takes practice," he would tell me. During one of our visits, he prodded at me to sketch a portrait of him. I tried as hard as I could on a piece of notebook paper that he gave me. He was proud of it, though I knew very well there was not much likeness to him at all in my sketch.

Poetry and short stories were also a part of my creative world back then.

A friend of mine encouraged me to submit one of them to a poetry contest he found in the back of a periodical.

I did, and to my surprise, a few weeks later, I received a check in the mail for $100 and rave reviews on the poem.

THINK ABOUT IT...

I am so grateful for people in my inner circle who have cheered me on to succeed.

Who is or has been your cheerleader? Is there someone you know who needs a cheerleader?

Each of us has been gifted with talents skills and abilities. God gives them to us at will.

Thankfully, He does not change His mind when He does. What are the gifts has He given you?

Seek Him for the platform to display your "art" and know that Papa God proudly displays the masterpiece He created-YOU.

Unfortunately, life and bad decisions robbed me of developing these gifts further. Which, unbeknownst to me, created a resolve that maybe it wasn't meant to be. That is until it was given the opportunity.

Our church was re-designing the walls of the children's church with flowers. I was pretty surprised by how alive my creativity was, even though I was rusty. With

Father, I ask You to reveal every gift You have deposited into me. I received them with open hands and understanding that Your gifts are not just for me to glean from and enjoy. In Jesus name, so be it.

James 1:17

each stroke of my paintbrushes dipped in lavender, blue, and yellow, creating the flowers on the wall, I pondered on this. I heard so clearly while painting, "See, it never went anywhere. I don't take back My gifts to you."

Since then, I have continued to grow and develop this creativity. So, Grandpa, this is for you. Thank you for believing in me! I love you, and I will see you soon!

_____

_____

_____

_____

_____

_____

_____

_____

_____

Expressway – The Door is Open, Come On In

My eyes popped open one morning, fresh from a dream I'd just had. I needed no explanation. I needed no interpretation. The details were solid, vivid, with simplistic symbolism that needed no breakdown. My faith was stirred just by falling asleep.

I stood at these huge solid wooden doors. It was one of those that would hurt your knuckles to knock with any effort. I knocked on it with all my might and felt like no one heard me knocking. I knocked until my eyes were directed to the keyed padlock at the top. Once I realized the key was around my wrist, I unlocked the lock, and the door swung wide open.

Inside was a huge warehouse full of large wooden barrels. They seemed as massive as the door. At least six feet tall and six feet wide. Each barrel had a label. The labels read "Healing," "Faith," "Wisdom," "Salvation," "Forgiveness," and the like. I didn't browse too long. There were barrels for what seemed like miles, and each filled to the brim with vibrant emerald, green "pods" that reminded me of detergent pods. I picked one up and held it to my heart. It instantly fused to my being.

The next thing I knew, I was back outside the closed door. The scene was time-lapsed of me opening the door by repeatedly unlocking the lock several times and then turning the knob and touching the door until the door was finally open for good. By this point, time slowed, and I realized a line of people forming waiting for their miracle.

THINK ABOUT IT...

I came to understand that my vision was skewed regarding having "all access" to heavenly promises.

I was looking through a beggar's lenses. The only key I need to open the door is faith.

What is keeping you from opening the door? What is it you need all access to?

Do you know someone else who could use an all-access pass to God's miracle warehouse?

Father, I thank You that the doors are open, and You have given me an all-access pass. I understand and receive the keys of faith to grab hold of all I need that is in You. You are a good Father, and You take care of Your children. In Jesus name, so be it.

Matthew 7:7-8

I would go in and grab their request as quickly as I could. Each walked away faith-filled and satisfied. People were piling up in the hallway until finally, I began to encourage each person, "Go get what you need. The door is open."

There was no bewilderment. No confusion. No asking for permission. "Come and get it. The Door is open."

_____

_____

_____

_____

_____

_____

_____

_____

_____

_____

_____

_____

Car Game – Dad's God Jokes

Have you ever heard a corny dad joke? I'm sure we all have. I've heard a few that are quite hilarious, in my opinion. A few of my favorites I heard from my dad. "Why did God make our butt-cracks vertical instead of horizontal? So, it wouldn't go "BUH-BUH-BUH" when we slide down the slide naked!" and "Why did God make the gorilla's nostrils so big? "Cause they got big fingers!"

Yeah, yeah. Okay, maybe these are not the funniest jokes. I, myself, love to laugh. But who doesn't, right? Growing up, my smile was something frequently commented on. I've been told I have a "Julia Roberts" smile, and I've been compared to the Joker from Batman. Smiling and laughter is a treasure to me. Scattered among many examples of heartache and pain are also many seeds of laughter. I've discovered laughing so hard I cry is something I miss. So, I am delighted to know God has a good sense of humor. And if there is any question about it, I can assure you He does.

Several years ago, I joined a gym. I was overweight, out of shape, and miserable. I went faithfully for several months, and the rewards were finally starting to show. I still had a long way to go, but a bit of confidence was beginning to grow. I had a friend who I considered to be knowledgeable in fitness, nutrition, and weight loss. She offered quite a bit of support, encouragement, and instruction to help me along the way. I truly honored her as a friend and mentor, so any advice she offered, I gladly accepted.

I've heard that sometimes when we wake up with a particular song stuck in our heads, it would behoove us to ask Holy Spirit why. Maybe, just maybe, it's the song that He would have us singing in worship to Him that day. I'm no scholar, but I did have a heart that desired to be

THINK ABOUT IT...

I believe we are all called to worship. Not just in a physical location at an appointed time, but in our daily lives.

I want to worship Him in the way I talk. In the way I work at my profession. In the way interact with people in public places. In my giving. In my attitude. In the way I love others.

Has God ever led you to worship in a manner that may have been out of your comfort zone?

How have you experienced the humor of God in your journey?

pleasing to God, so I went to work one day (as a charge nurse in a nursing home) with a Christian song about dancing for the Lord stuck in my head.

I can be candid and transparent to admit that singing is NOT one of my gifts or talents. I could be even more transparent and acknowledge that I can't carry a tune in a bucket even if my life depended on it. However, the Bible says to make a joyful noise. It doesn't say anything about it having to sound good. So, I obediently sang this song as I worked. "Dance! Dance! Let the Spirit move you!"

I caught a giggle from several of my coworkers and residents as I sang throughout the day. I sang at the nurses' station. I sang as I pushed my big ole med cart down my wing. I sang as I carried lunch trays in the dining room. No fear. I sang out loud, and I was happy to do it. Even though everyone must've thought I'd lost my mind.

The buzz of call lights ringing, steady flow of doctors' orders and phone calls left me exhausted as usual by the end of the day. I came home from work, peeled off my scrubs, showered, and made dinner for the kids. By the time I got to the gym later that evening, I had forgotten all about that song. I met up with my friend, and together we did some cardio, worked our arms and back, and planned to take a cycling class. But by the time we got there, the class was full. The only other class available was, wait for it—Zumba.

Want more transparency? Here it is. I dance worse than I sing. I stood there by the entrance to the Zumba room with my friend, waiting for an answer. I tried my best to avoid what was sure to be an awkward situation. I really tried to get out of it. I made up excuses. I promised to go another time. But my friend was persistent, so I decided to suck it up, plaster a fake smile on my face and get in there and Zumba.

The room had mirrors on all four walls, and I was literally the biggest girl in the room. Much younger gals than myself surrounded me. Who, by the way, was in much better shape and looked a hundred times better in spandex? And, of course, they made Zumba look easy.

I put my best foot forward. I dipped. I stooped. I swayed. I swung my jumbo-gigantic, baby-birthing hips to the left and the right. I mean, I cha-cha'd for as long as I could. I tried my hardest to keep up. I could feel sweat beading up in places I'd rather not mention. My face felt hot. I felt every ounce of my body fat jiggle and wiggle and move in ways I have never imagined.

About halfway through the class, I finally got a good look at myself in the mirror doing the Zumba dance, and I could not help but laugh inside.

I chuckled and thought, "Now God, You know that no self-respecting Jesus-loving Christian lady ought to be seen in public movin' around and looking like this." The humor in my own tone still brings a smile to my face. I continued on-trying not to look at myself in the mirror, but I couldn't help but to look. I couldn't help but to laugh at myself. I was making up my own dance moves because I couldn't keep up with everyone else. Finally, I was out of breath and decided I needed a break. I excused myself from the group for a drink of water. I picked up my bottle and started to chug when I heard that song again in my head: "Dance! Dance!" Followed by a very humorous Holy Spirit whisper, "Gotcha!"

Yeah, Dad, You got jokes.

Father, I thank You that have worked out every single detail in my life, even as I worship You in my "day to day" routines. I can enjoy Your presence at any time because You are with me in my worship. Help me to experience every facet of Your personality, including Your sense of humor. In Jesus name, so be it.

Romans 12:1-2

_____

_____

_____

_____

Exhaust - Eww, I Dealt It

I stood there at the altar, excited for the impartation I was about to receive. Who doesn't love an amazing guest revivalist from Australia, right? I practically tripped myself to get up there as fast as I did. Baby did that man tap me on the head and tell God, "Get her, God. Triple anointing." I fell backward immediately in response. Stayed down only a second and popped right back up. He came back around, and I blurted out, "One more round!" Bam! I was out. I laid out on the floor of our church and shook under the power of God.

Once I made it back to my seat, I kept smelling the sweetest scent. It reminded me of frankincense, but it smelled much purer. I sniffed around on my clothes, on my neighbor to my right and my left. After a few seconds, the scent would leave. I was aware I might have forgotten my deodorant. Then it would return. I must have seemed like a mad woman sniffing everyone around me. Finally, the lady sitting to my right asked, "What are you doing?" I replied to her, "You don't smell that? Something smells so good! Where is it coming from?"

"No," she said, "I think it's just for you. Enjoy it." And I did. I certainly did not want to have to sit there and smell my own armpit funk. A few weeks later, I was at a woman's conference. Toward the end of the night, I was face down in worship. The pastor, who was walking by, stopped, and stood next to me. She said as she breathed in deep, "Oh, that smells good. I know Papa is enjoying your worship." I knew the scriptural reference and understood what she was picking up. She explained to everyone, "Sometimes God will let me smell the fragrances when we worship.

And it doesn't always smell good. Sometimes it smells like

I learned two important lessons in this experience:

1. When my heart is pure, my worship is a sweet aroma in the nostrils of God. It smells beautifully delicious.
2. When my heart is not pure puffed up in pride or unforgiveness (or a host of other mess) my worship stinks to high heaven. Literally.

If you could smell your own worship, what might it smell like?

rotten eggs."

Well, I got up off the floor feeling some kind of special. A few minutes later, as I "worshipped," I smelled what she was talking about. It was quite disgusting. I almost blamed it on somebody else. Nope, whoever smelt it, dealt it.

And as I used to tell my kids, when I smelled something funky, somebody forgot to wipe. Yep, another heart check. That was embarrassing.

Father, I repent of every time I offered You stinky worship full of "me". I receive Your forgiveness and ask that would quicken my spirit any time in the future and redirect my heart towards the only One worthy to praised. You. You alone are God, and I am thankful for all You have done for me. In Jesus name, so be it.

Isaiah 64:6

Yielding the Right of Way: Jar of Pickles

Momma Linda, a woman I greatly admire, once taught me how to handle offense. If anyone has walked with Jesus any length of time, we know offenses will come. It is in our hands how to handle them. This woman of great wisdom shared how a jar of pickles saved her from unforgiveness settling in her heart. It was as simple as a jar of pickles. And the most impactful part for me was hearing her say, "What happens next is none of your business," as she shook her hand with one finger pointing at me. Meaning, what goes on in the other person's heart is none of our concern. We are to do our part and leave the outcome to God. Well, soon enough, I would have to make my own jar of pickles. But I am not much of a cook.

"Hey," he responded when I answered the phone. "You need to teach your boys not to mess around with guns. Your son took the bullets out of my gun and put the safety on." He was speaking of my eldest son, who was eleven at the time. Just this sentence alone was enough to send this momma bear reeling.

We were visiting some folks (and that is as much as I would like to expound on for privacy) when this event occurred. We spent the whole day at their home watching movies and eating dinner. We weren't the only visitors. There was also another young woman with her three-year-old daughter. The kids played all afternoon. All in all, I'd say we had a nice day. And then halfway home, I get this phone call.

"Where was it?" I asked. Expecting an answer like, in a drawer in their bedroom or closet. "It's a rifle, and it was in the office behind the door." There was a playroom with a tv and video game console in the next room, and all four of the kids played in the back part of the house with little supervision. The adults were mainly in the front part of the house, as we usually would be. I was aware of a gun safe that was always locked and secure. However, I was completely unaware of a loaded, unlocked, and accessible rifle.

Naturally (in my opinion), I replied, "Okay, but let me get this straight. There was a loaded rifle out and unattended when there are children in the house?"

I quickly discovered that was the wrong thing to say, and a heated argument broke loose. I argued that my children are children. And as any child would, my child made a childish decision that could have cost a life. A life I was not willing to put at risk ever again if their guns were not properly secured. He argued that it is his home, his rifle, and he can keep it anywhere he wants. I need to teach my kids not to play with guns. While I did speak at length to all three of my boys about guns and gun safety, I was really upset that my children had access to a

Father, reveal any person I have been holding offense toward. I understand the sacrifice that Jesus made for me, therefore I must not harbor unforgiveness in my heart. Show me what You would have me to present as a love offering so that I may be free. I understand that what happens after I present that love offering is none of my business, but rather, Yours to handle. In Jesus name, so be it.

James 12:14-21

loaded weapon. I was so angry. I vowed that not only would my kids never touch their guns ever again, but we would not be over their house anymore either.

And so it went, weeks went by, and I had nothing left to say about the matter. Until that is, I began to feel convicted for harboring offense, and I was reminded to bring them a jar of pickles.

The boys and I were starting to miss our fellowship with these folks, and I decided it was time to put the argument to bed. I shopped all afternoon for the perfect peace offering since I hadn't the first clue how to make pickles. I finally settled on a wooden figurine. It was about a foot long, maybe five inches tall— three wooden monkeys sitting on a log that read, "Hear no evil. See no evil. Speak no evil." I thought it was cute. I wrote a simple note to apologize for my behavior, stating that we could agree to disagree. I presented my peace offering and humbled myself. Soon after, I received a call from the missus, and we were invited to their home for thanksgiving. I accepted the invitation.

Soon after we got there, on the shelf above their tv was the figurine I bought. No words were spoken between us about what took place, but I did sneak a peak in the back part of the house. I checked the office. The gun safe was closed-up tight. I checked behind the door. No gun. I checked in the other rooms, none. Thank You, Holy Spirit, our jar of pickles did the trick.

_____

_____

_____

_____

_____

_____

_____

_____

_____

_____

_____

_____

_____

_____

Driver's Ed: Out of Lodebar

I'm no biblical scholar by any means. I never went to seminary. I am not fluent in biblical terminology. Nor am I an avid historian who regularly studies root words and their origins while I read. Though I confess, these are admirable qualities worth asking God for, and I do. I read the Word of God, and sometimes a single word will drop into my spirit and stir up my curiosity. Such was the case when I heard the word "Lodebar."

To my best recollection, I was finally exiting a self-described desert wandering era. More accurate, an adult-sized hissy fit. I was alive again. Everything was as fresh to my spirit as it was the day I was born again. If you have ever been one to buy new undies and can't wait to go home and slip on a pair of the freshest, cutest, form-fitting, brand-spankin new underwear, that's what it felt like. Come on. I'm not the only gal who does that!

My finances needed a major make-over at the time. I bring that up because, well, this is how ignorant I was. Payday was a few days away. My pantry needed filling in the worse way. As I was going through the pantry and making my grocery list, I heard, "I'm taking you out of Lodebar."

I knew I'd heard that word before, and it was in the bible. So, I look it up. And praise God, I went to my local Food Town to fill up my grocery basket, knowing somebody would gift me some groceries. I still chuckle when I think about that. Imagine my surprise when I had to swipe my debit card.

Up to this point in my journey, I experienced such tender moments with the Holy Spirit and God's goodness. I cannot ever accurately describe the thankfulness I feel towards Him and the strong desire to give it back. This was my prayer. "God, I want to do great things for You."

Sometime later, I received a prophetic word. In summary, it was, "God is about to drop a huge amount of provision in your lap. Don't squander it, don't waste it. When it's time, He will show you what to do with it." I believe this word is still being unpacked. Soon after, I asked a woman I greatly admire, Pam, to be my spiritual mamma. I had a dream. Unbeknownst to be, that dream would serve as both a confirmation to her and an invitation to me. The provision for deeper revelation, insight, transfer of anointing, operating in the gifts, and Godly

Father, I thank You that You desire to take me out of lack in every area. I don't care how You choose to do it. I stand before You boldly with an open heart and open hands, ready to receive. In Jesus name, so be it.

Philippians 4:19

leadership skills required to lead a movement at my doorstep—School of the Supernatural Ministry. Over the next three years, I would complete the first-year term under the leadership of my new Momma, complete the second year at another campus, and finally, teach the second year alongside Pam.

I love and honor you, Pam. I pray this book blesses you. I would not be where I am right now if not for your obedience to the call of God on your life. It has been a pleasure being your spiritual daughter and partner. I look forward to many more years of growth and fruitful friendship.

Sight Seeing - The Mountains

In 2013, I wanted more than anything to go on a mission trip, to explore our planet, reach God's people, and make a difference in someone else's life. My new friend and sister in Christ went on one, and I envied her experience. Not in a negative way, but my heart was newly opened to all what "ifs" that may present themselves in the future. I yearned for God to use me both at home and abroad. My heart was

healed of so much hurt and rejection.

I was finally beginning to see myself clearly through Jesus' lenses. Thus, I welcomed any opportunities to share my testimony. This is still true for me today.

Finally, my first mission trip opportunity made its way to my heart, and I was all in. Anticipation built over the coming months as the financial blessings arrived. I prayed and prayed, preparing the ground for Holy Spirit and me to work in.

I would spend an entire week with American missionaries Jerry and Carla Mansee, who faithfully served Jesus in Cuidad Victoria, Mexico. A lot of "firsts" happened for me

THINK ABOUT IT...

How dare I ever question what the hand of God can do?

Is there anything impossible, anything too grand for the hand of God?

Are there any mountains He can't move?

Have you ever been faced with this realization?

What mountain do you need to be removed in your life?

What mountain do you need help navigating around or over?

during this adventure. My first plane ride. My first public speaking assignment. And my first time praying for someone who succumbed to Holy Spirit by being "slain in the Spirit," which, by the way, was amazing to me due to language barriers. (Thankfully, Holy Spirit has no boundaries. It was utterly amazing. We visited many different places to minister: a drug rehab, an orphanage, a tent revival meeting, and several small village churches.

Father, open the eyes to my heart. Give me eyes to see what Holy Spirit wants me to see in this hour. No matter what mountain I may face, it is no challenge for You. In Jesus name, so be it.

Matthew 17:20

Many salvations, re-dedications, and deliverances took place. Oh, how delicious is the love of God poured out over His children! All of this was so much for me to take in. I journaled every sweet, delightful moment I could recall immediately upon arrival back to their home.

Their home, by the way, sat directly behind a massive mountain range. During one of our travels, Jerry drove us through them to take the scenic route. Their car was nothing fancy, a small sedan with a cassette player. I sat alone in the backseat as they played their worship music on the cassette. "Open the Eyes of My Heart." If there were any other songs on that tape, I never heard them. As that song played and I took in the magnificent beauty of those mountains, my heart was touched. I had what I can only describe as an open vision.

A vision of the hand of God "playing in the dirt." I was privy, right there in the back seat of an old sedan, to watch as a wonderfully breathtaking mountainous landscape was formed effortlessly by the Hand of the Most High, like a child playing in the dirt. "Open the eyes of my heart, Lord," I quietly sang as He continued to mold these tiny little mounds of dirt into massive mountain ranges. I could not help but weep as I watched. I thought, "How dare I ever question what the hand of God can do? Is there anything impossible, anything too grand for the hand of God? Are there any mountains He can't move?"

Yes, Lord. Open the eyes of my heart.

Setting the Time – "Wait" is a Four-Letter Word?

Years ago, when my boys were little, I stepped out of my house at 6:30 with a toddler on one arm and a diaper bag wrapped around the other while I helped my six-year-old down the steps. At the time, I worked in the mailroom of one of the downtown buildings and had a timeline to beat. Nobody likes driving in rush hour traffic. I was wearing my favorite black low-cut boots with tall heels. I hurried across the lawn to load up when my foot caught the corner of the sidewalk. Down I went. I had to turn with the fall to protect my son; otherwise, I would have crushed him. Long story short-my hurry cost me six weeks in a special boot.

If I learned anything in life—carrying rejection while believing for acceptance is about as easy as toting an infant in a car seat with a toddler on your hip while holding on to the hand of your five-year-old without dropping the diaper bag. To my dismay, it turns out that I know all too much about both and mastered neither. My own futile attempts have shattered both acceptance and my right ankle.

The invitation to be a daughter of the King was exciting in and of itself because light filled my heart. I felt a freedom I had not experienced before. My relationship with my Dad and I was being healed in such a beautiful way, a way I never thought I would see. I was beginning to experience the favor of God like I never experienced before. It was delicious. Seriously, I could get fat on it.

God was stirring up gifts inside of me. A fire was burning to step into the fullness of my destiny. I felt like I was at a buffet, and I was going home with it all. I kept hearing my spiritual leaders say, "It's a process." "It's not time yet."

THINK ABOUT IT...

A "not now" answer is not a "no." This was a hard lesson for me.

I've learned there is more than one answer for our prayers: yes, no, I've got something better, not now.

Can you think of a time you mistook a "not now" answer for a "no"?

Or a "no, I have something better," answer for a flat "no"?

Father, I thank You that all things are in Your hands. I understand "all things" includes Your plans for my life. Forgive me for any impatience I may have felt during the process. Help me to rest in knowing You are not time restrained. In Jesus name, so be it.

Philippians 4:6-7

"You aren't ready yet." "If God launched you out right now, you would fall flat on your face."

Pam said something once after a prayer meeting that has stuck with me all this time. She said, "Katherine, you have an amazing call of God on your life. It is there. I can see it. You have a huge platform ahead of you. But you are in training. You are in training for reigning. Don't try to make things happen. I see you in a crockpot. God is doing a deep work in you, a long-lasting work. It is full coursework but in a slow cooker, and you are not done yet. You will be an arrow in the quiver and shot out in His timing, not yours. Enjoy the journey."

But since when was "wait" a four-letter word?

_____

_____

_____

_____

_____

_____

_____

_____

_____

_____

License and Registration-My Father Named Me

God has done so much for me. There are no words to describe the depth of gratefulness I feel when I think about it. I understand why the leper came back to give thanks to Jesus. I cannot imagine not returning thanks. It runs deep and is now a huge part of who I am. How can it not be? After getting such a gift, who would want to toss it aside and not offer every part of my life as a thank offering? Exactly.

"God, I give my life to You as a thank offering. Use me, Father. I want to do great things for You. I want to be a vessel, You can use to bring more Glory to Your Name. You have done so much for me. I can never repay You. God, I want to do great things for You. I was weak, and You made me strong. I was wounded, and You healed me. I needed Love, and You poured it out thick like honey all over me. God, I want to do great things for You. I was dirty, and You made me clean. I was angry. You gave me Peace. You taught me how to forgive. God, I want to do great things for You. I needed a Father, and You were there. I needed a Healer. You were there. I needed a purpose. You gave me a purpose. I needed a Friend. You are my Friend. I could not trust, but You taught me I could trust You. I needed a Defender, and

THINK ABOUT IT...

I have had many prayers that were just between God and me.

Many He answers in such an intimate way to let me know He heard me.

Have you experienced this tender side of Jesus in His response to your prayer?

I can see the fingerprints of Jesus all over my life as I give Him thanks for all He has done.

What is your prayer of thankfulness?

Do you know who He made YOU to be?

You came to my rescue. God, I want to do Great things for You. Everyone I loved left me. You never left me. Everyone I trusted lied to me. But You never lie. My plans always failed. Your plans never fail. God, I want to do great things for You. I walked away from You. You came running after me. I needed to be loved. Your Love is powerful. I could not see. You opened my eyes. God, I want to do great things for You. I needed an identity. You gave me a new name. God, I want to do great things for You."

I yearned most of my entire life for identity. For purpose. For meaning. After all my failed attempts at finding it in dark places, I did not have much of an identity at all. I was a walking dead woman until I met Jesus and life began to fill my lungs. "God, I want to do great things for You."

"God, I want to do great things for You." This has become my prayer. I had never said that out loud to anyone before. I did not need to. I know He hears me.

I went to a women's retreat in October 2014 known as Drenched. I knew most of the women who attended. I attend church with several of them, and only a few were a part of my inner circle. The majority were from Portland, Seattle, or Memphis. Prior to our arrival, the leaders wrote all the attendee's name on a piece of paper to pray and prophesy over.

At the close of the first night of the Drenched weekend, all the women received prayer. When it was my turn, these words were spoken over me, "Katherine, I saw this name, and I could not pronounce your last name. But God said her last name is Great. Catherine, the Great. She does not need a last name; it is Great. She will do Great things for Me." No surprise, I fell to the floor and wept with even greater thankfulness that God heard my prayer, and He answered with a YES. The

Father, I pour out my thanks to You for all You have done for me. I thank You that You knew be even when I was in my mother's belly and You pre-ordained me to do great things for You. May my praise for all You have done be brought to forefront to share Your goodness to the world. In Jesus name, so be it.

Jeremiah 1:5

prophetic word continued, and those words I hold tightly even to this day.

When I arrived home, I called my dad in excitement of what happened. I told him everything. My prayers, the depth of gratitude for what He has done in my life. And I told him about my new name. "Well, sugar, don't you know I named you?" he asked. "Well, yeah, I know. Mom was going to name me Sonia." I replied. My dad chuckled again, "No, I mean, I chose your name. I knew you would be different, and I wanted a strong name for you. So, I named you Katherine, after Catherine the Great." Yes, before I was even born, my Father named me.

Driving with Dad - Father's Embrace

My Dad and I 1976

I love my dad. Let me say that again. I love my dad. When I think of Papa God, I think of my dad. I get teary-eyed when I really focus on the heart of the Father. It's pure. It's deep. It's a forever love.

I can picture myself approaching Him. I'm about eight years old, with short brown hair, freckles, and a toothy smile. He leans forward with inviting open arms that emphatically imply, "Come to Me." I run to him with my awkward trot and leap to His lap. I always (in my mind's eye) see my dad's face and the love that I see in the Father's eyes and feel of His embrace that can only compare to my dad. I know our earthly-human love pales in comparison to Agape Love, and there is no perfect way to describe the intensity.

I hadn't always been able to make the "Father" connection. The eight-year-old me wore some deceitful lenses that ultimately caused me to believe God was an angry cement-looking giant with a huge hammer in his hands waiting to whack me upside the head and throw me out.

Let me explain. One day my family was visiting my

THINK ABOUT IT...

Sometimes our life experiences skew our perception of how God see's us.

It's important, critical even, that we identify false lenses quickly if we truly want to grow and develop in the things of God.

When you think of Father God, what comes to mind? Do you see, as I did at first a mean old man waiting to whack you once upside the head? Or do you see a loving set of arms wooing you to His lap?

What is your perception of the Father?

Ask Him to show You how He sees You.

grandparents. There were aunts, uncles, and cousins everywhere. I caught a glimpse of my dad standing out in the front yard chatting with one of my uncles. He stood tall and poised with folded arms. The sun was beaming down, and his shadow seemed to stretch for miles. I remember looking at him a few feet away and suddenly being overcome with a craving for affection from him. I don't know what sparked it, though I suspect it might have been the sight of my male cousins and their dads bonding nearby.

I was a timid child, but somehow, I worked up the courage to approach dad's shadow and attempted to sneak in a brief hug. With a short pat on the back and an abrupt "go play," I slinked away, feeling utterly rejected and choking back tears. I could hear an inner voice whisper (convincingly, I might add), "He doesn't love you."

I remember this ten-second memory like it was ten seconds ago. I carried it into my teenage and young adult years. Unfortunately, this deception caused a lot of heartaches before I was finally born again. It took a deep intimate SOZO moment of healing to separate perception and truth through the corrective lenses of Holy Spirit.

I was repeatedly lied to. My dad and I have had several intimate conversations since then. I can see and feel the intensity of the love he has for me and the

Father, I thank You that You are not a mean Father. You are kind, loving, tender, and You are waiting on me to come running to You. I understand that I can enter into Your presence, sit in Your lap, and hear Your heart for me. Speak to me Father, as my Daddy, my Pappa who love knows no bounds. What do You want me to know? In Jesus name, so be it.

2 Corinthians 6:18

sorrow that one of his own children ever believed wasn't loved and accepted by him. I am wrecked by it, especially now that the truth has been exposed and having made the connection to the Father's love.

My dad loves me. My Father loves me. I can and do experience the Father's embrace in all its fullness, and in His presence. I can come running with absolutely no fear of ever being turned away.

_____

_____

_____

_____

_____

_____

_____

_____

_____

_____

_____

_____

_____

_____

_____

_____

_____

_____

_____

_____

Better Days

Major Lane Changes – Green Light?

"God, please. You know my heart. I need out. Please, I feel Your hand has lifted, and the grace is gone from me here. Would you please show me the green light? I will be on my way. You give me the courage to make the jump, and I will jump. You know my heart. You know how much these last ten years have impacted me both positively and negatively. I only want to be where You take me.

I cannot do this alone. I know You did not bring me this far to watch me fail. I need Your guidance. You know all the firsts I have experienced here—my first major career in my life. You gave me the courage to jump into nursing school. You brought me through it with flying colors. You opened doors I could have never opened by myself. You gave me this job. You knew what You were doing when I stepped into these doors. You knew I would love it.

You watched me as I grew into the nurse I have become. You helped me get through mistakes, deaths, and you helped me make lasting relationships with co-workers. You have seen every tear I ever cried. You see it all—the good, the bad, and the ugly. You see it all. Every time I was mocked. Every time I was lied on. Every time I was accused of something, I did not do. Hear my heart, Father.

I thank You for the peace that comes knowing You are on the move. Show me the green light and help me to jump." I prayed this kind of prayer fervently over my career for the last ten or so months of my first nursing job. I worked there for ten years. When that green light finally shone, walking out of those doors was such a relief.

THINK ABOUT IT...

God is concerned about everything that concerns us. We can trust Him in our unknown.

Can you recall a time in your life where you knew you were at a crossroads?

How did He show you which way to turn? Did you see Him when you got there?

Father, I thank You that You are good Father, and I can trust You in my unknown. I know You will be there beside me as I take steps in faith, and You will also be waiting on the other side.

Habakkuk 3:19

I did so with peace and an inner knowing, "My Daddy has got me in His hands, and I will be okay."

I was okay! I found another job within a few weeks. Too bad I was not finished with making that lane change when floodwaters started building up on unfamiliar streets. Somehow, the streetlamp of Holy Spirit was leading on the side streets to a bigger blessing. I simply couldn't see the signs yet.

_____

_____

_____

_____

_____

_____

_____

_____

_____

_____

_____

_____

_____

_____

Driving in the Rain: Better Days

It was Friday afternoon. After work, I did what I was supposed to do. I braved the busy aisles of my local Wal-Mart to buy up essentials to weather the storm. I bought water, sodas, chips, cookies, canned goods, and all those rainy-day comfort foods we all rush out to buy when a big storm is headed our way. Yes, how smart of me.

"Mom, should we get some sandbags for the doors, just in case?" Gabriel asked. Silly boy. "No, we will get a lot of rain, but I'm sure that'll be it," I replied. Indeed, we did get a lot of rain when Harvey came through.

Saturday, it rained sporadically throughout the day. A few heavy downpours, but mostly drizzle—just enough cloud cover to keep the sunlight beaming from down on a late-August day. But we went about our day-to-day as usual, and by the time we went to bed, most of our goodies were gone. By midnight, the rain picked up, and I was sound asleep. (Enter my stupidity right here.) I was awakened by the absence of the steady whir of my box fan. I believed it to be that our power went out. That would have been an intelligent assumption, but when I heard the tv playing in the living room, I knew I was wrong.

And oh, how wrong I was! I no sooner gave my usual hand wave to Jesus, sat up, and swung my feet off the bed and onto the floor when reality quickly set in. My feet were met with wet carpet. Correction met with almost seven inches of rainwater all through my house. Sheer panic was starting to take root. I waded through the house to discover my tile flooring from room to room like driftwood. I opened the front door only to discover my car was almost completely submerged as it was parked in the street. By the time all three of my children were awake, I

THINK ABOUT IT...

God did not promise us everything would be gravy during our time on earth. He warns us of the opposite. But, to survive the storm, we must keep our eyes on Him even if we can't see Him in our boat.

I prayed once, "Father, give me storm-sleeping peace like Jesus had in the boat."

I believe He answered that prayer for me in these few minutes standing in my sister's garage. It felt incredible.

Have you had a major storm hit your life? How did the flood waters reach your heart?

Was you able to say from your heart: God, You are still good?"

was frantic. I probably said more curse words in those first few minutes than I had since I'd been born again. My oldest son, thankfully, stepped to the plate and gathered the four of us in prayer.

Once peace settled in the house, we began making plans for our immediate escape. It was still pouring rain, and the water was slowly rising throughout the house. I called my dad to let him know what was going on. I called my sister, who lived up the street from me. Her home was free and clear of any flooding. The kids and I packed a few items in plastic bags, and we swam our way to my sister's house. Standing in their garage, we watched as the back half of our street slowly accrued more rainwater. We watched as we literally saw fish swimming in the street.

The rain continued to pour over the next 24 hours, but the flooding receded well before noon on Sunday. My house took in almost a foot of water. My sister and I went through the house to begin the grueling cleanup process. We pulled up carpet, tile, and floor trim as best we could to prevent any molding that was sure to follow. Though it continued to rain, my neighborhood did not flood again. Several other areas did flood, even worse than ours over the following days. The amount of damage done in my home was nothing compared to what was to come for others. Even two-story homes were devastated by Harvey's rain.

That Sunday evening, I stood in my sister's garage watching the rain. I must have had a million things running through my mind. An endless to-do list was growing by the hour: call FEMA, call my home insurance company, call my mortgage company, and file a claim with my auto insurance company.

Go and buy bleach, mops, sponges, more trash bags, and rewash all the clothes—drill home to the kids the importance of their help in the dreaded clean-up process.

Images of things I held close to my heart came to mind when I realized they are now garbage. The bible I read every morning with years of sideline notes, prayers, revelation, and tears was ruined. Study books I used almost every day were also destroyed. Furniture gifted to me that belonged to a patient I cared for was now trash.

But as I stood there in her garage watching the rain, I felt an overwhelming peace fall on me. As tears fell, I was reminded once again of His goodness towards me, and all I could say was, "You're still good, God. You're still good." I was alive. My kids were alive. We were safe. My sister was safe. And God is still on the throne of

Heaven. Though everything I owned was about to be in garbage bags and piled up in heaps, I was soaking in Peace.

"You're still good, God," I told Him over and over in the garage that evening. He would orchestrate yet another "re-build" in my life. He did it before. He'll do it again. I knew He would.

Father, You are good. You are enough. No matter what storm I go through, I am not going through it alone. Help me to see You sleeping in my boat while we ride this storm out together. You are good. In Jesus name, so be it.

Matthew 8:23-27

_____

_____

_____

_____

_____

_____

_____

_____

_____

_____

_____

_____

_____

Turn Around, Don't Drown - When it Rains, it Pours

THINK ABOUT IT...

One of my mentors, Momma Pam, once told me "Whenever you are up against something you have never been through, ask God, "What do You want me to know about You I have not experienced before?"

Indeed, I have seen Him as my Best Friend, as my Comforter, as my Provider, as my Healer. This was a new area for me.

How have you experienced Him as your Best Friend? Comforter? Provider? Healer? Defender?

It's easy to run in fear. It takes strength and courage to seek Him for a new opportunity to know Him on a deeper level.

Yes, when it rains, it pours. How true that statement is sometimes. If you live anywhere near the Gulf Coast, I am sure you can agree. Summertime and hurricane seasons have the potential to threaten our livelihood. On the heels of a devastating storm, Harvey was another storm much more personal to me.

Harvey made his rude arrival in my life in August 2017. I woke up to almost a foot of water in my home. A home that I worked my tail off to provide for my family. I furnished it shortly after we moved in. Everything in our home had great personal value to me. Primarily because of how it was birthed. The modest little home God blessed us with was a great testimony to the restoration process He brought us through. Yet after Harvey, it felt like I had to do it all over again.

My boys and I lived with my sister and her family for three months while we did the grueling work of cleaning up the damage done by this storm. On top of working a full-time job and the kids returning to school, we spent countless hours of labor doing the following: trim and sheetrock removal, deep cleaning, sweeping, mopping, pulling nails, cutting, and placing insulation, caulking, scrubbing, rinse and repeat, then back to my sister's house to bathe and get ready to do it all over again the next day.

I would be lying through my teeth if I said my joy stayed at a healthy and robust "10" every day on the 1-10 joy scale. In fact, it was a difficult couple of months. We had days of disappointment. Days of discouragement. Days of waiting with our hands seemingly tied as we waited for contractors to finish on their end. We were guests in my sister's home, and while they never showed any annoyance of us living there by the end of November, we were ready to move back into our home even if it was not "move-in-ready," and we did just that.

The floors were not complete. We were still walking on a bare concrete floor. We did not have beds. We were gifted a pull-out sofa bed with a love seat, and I bought some air mattresses for the boys. Our refrigerator was in our living room, and we had one working toilet, but hey, we were home. I was finally starting to feel like I could breathe again.

Then December came.

I was still going to church, still praying, and still serving in what small capacity I had for the time being. In fact, I was looking forward to what December would bring. I was all set to fly out to Portland, Oregon, for the Her Voice Conference. I felt honored to serve and be a part of the ministry team. I bought some new clothes. I bought a nice coat. I had my suitcase packed, and everything was in order. A fresh outpouring of Agape love was all I craved. Excitement was building in my heart again. I was all set to head out to the airport the following day, and nothing could have squashed that excitement. Nothing that is, until I opened a letter from the Board of Nursing.

(When I reflect on this time period, I wish I could tell you that my faith was at an all-time high. I wished I could say that I walked in peace every moment. I would like to say I walked and lived like Jesus through it all. But that is so far from the truth.

I sat on my couch with this letter in my hand, literally trembling in complete shock at what I was reading. In only a few short seconds, every ounce of excitement I had was replaced by fear. In short, this letter explained that an investigation was in progress into an incident that had occurred a few years prior. I was aware of the events and circumstances in question, and the details were still fresh in my mind. The letter outlined the process of the investigation, the next steps I needed to take, and a general guideline of how the process works.

Friends, the devil does not play fair at all. Admittedly, fear took root in my heart. It was as if I already had one broken leg, and in an instant, I had two broken legs and a few fractured ribs. I knew there was a chance my nursing career could be over, and that alone ushered a dark cloud of unnecessary shame and embarrassment that followed me for the next six months.

I did everything the letter instructed me to do. I submitted a statement and provided letters from previous bosses and outstanding employee reviews to speak on my nursing skills, integrity, and compassion for my patients. I prayed—a lot. I cried—a lot. The attack on my mind was awful.

"You are not a good nurse, and soon everyone will know it."

"You are not going to have that license very much longer, and then what are you going to do?"

"You will lose your job. Your house."

"You are such a fake. Look at you. You are weak."

But God! So far in my journey with Jesus, I had come to know Him as my Savior. As my Teacher. As my Father. As my Healer. As my Provider. As my Friend. I was about to know Him as my Defender. Though that ugly cloud thundered and made threats, I countered with, "I am a Child and a Daughter of the Most High. Jesus is the Great Defender. He is my Attorney." If I said this once, I said it a thousand times. Sometimes I said it full of faith, sometimes, not so much.

I remember one Sunday morning (after about five months in) during worship, I heard Holy Spirt say to me, "I've got this, Katherine. I have already done it. It's done. I've got it." I remember it so clearly because this was the first time in this situation that I could "see" it before my natural eyes could see it. I could see the stamp of dismissal on the whole investigation.

Those fiery darts still came, but my response never changed. "Devil, you are a liar. I have the best Defender, and it has already been taken care of."

Yes, indeed. I have the Best Defender. Thank You. Case dismissed.

Father, I thank You there are more than one way to experience Your goodness. Remind me when I face foreign situations to seek a new dimension of Your character and Your love for me. In Jesus name, so be it.

Psalms 25:4-5

_____
_____
_____
_____
_____
_____
_____
_____
_____
_____
_____
_____
_____

Stranded– There's Safety in Numbers

"Sugar, you need to get back in church. I'm not telling you anything you don't already know. That's where your strength is. I have always admired your faith. You are the daughter I never had to worry about in that area, but right now, sugar, you need to be where your strength is."

These are the words from my daddy while I was vacationing in the desert. Correction: vacationing in the desert with no water, wind, or ac. I chose to camp out there. I knew he was right. Of course, I knew he was right. Even though these words came from the man whose best excuse NOT to go to church was "I don't have any clean pants to wear." (Which I sarcastically replied, "You mean to tell me your answer to Jesus when He comes back will be "Well, I'm sorry Jesus, I didn't have any clean britches to wear?" I love you, Daddy! And thank you for not giving up on praying for me).

While it took me a little longer than I care to admit, I eventually made my way back into the fold. Step by step, prayer by prayer!

September 10, 2018

"Just get back up again." These are the words I hear in my head-the prayer I wanted to pray out loud at church. "Here I am. Help me to make the first step. Here I am; what now?" I heard and felt this silent prayer from the pit of my innermost being.

Then Anita came to pray for me. I let the words reach my tongue, and my sobbing, sorrowful voice followed. That felt so good. I didn't know what Your answer would be. I didn't know anything at that moment, except I wanted to join You again and partner with You in my life again.

THINK ABOUT IT...

If the enemy can get us isolated, he can back us into a corner. If we let the enemy back us into a corner, we are at his mercy. But God.

When I speak of "the church," I don't necessarily mean a physical building. Not entirely anyway. I pushed good friends and mentors out of my sphere of influence. That was not a good move on my part.

Thankfully, I have amazing parents, mentors and pastors who never stopped praying for me.

The enemy thought he had an ace in the hole, but God the last word.

Why does the enemy try to use isolation as a tactic?

What is your defense?

Have you ever been tempted to pull away from your church family when faced with trouble?

I cried. I cried a lot. I wept. Hard. Loud. All of everything I've kept pushing underneath for months.

It just burst out.

Today is Monday. I'm not sure of how that heart surgery took place yesterday at the altar, but I walked away with an assurance that Your promises are still there. That I can and will get back up again. That most of all, Your love for me has not changed.

Today is Monday. I feel lighter still.

I still have not processed all the things or places I've allowed myself to sink into. I am sure I have work to do, but I am at peace in that if I do my part, You will be right beside me to do Yours.

I lied when I said, "I don't want ministry." I do.

One thing I can say, I am humbled by this season. To know I am human with flesh that stinks to high heaven and reeks of sin and shame. Who am I except a daughter rescued once again from my own prison? I am no better than anyone else. I think back to my own ego. How mightily I thought of myself. Oh, no, ma'am.

I am a daughter saved by grace through Your mercy. Just because You love me, and nothing more.

Thank you, Anita, for your obedience, kindness, wisdom, and impartation.

I love my church family!

_____

_____

_____

_____

_____

_____

_____

_____

Father, I thank You for my local church and church family. I bless my pastors, mentors, and brothers and sisters in Christ. I ask that You help me to stand against any tactic the enemy may use to keep me from coming together in fellowship and prayer with the church family You have provided for me. In Jesus name, so be it.

Hebrews 10:12

_____

_____

_____

_____

_____

_____

_____

_____

_____

_____

No Parking Zones - She's a Dirty Birdie

Don't judge me! During the absolute worst of my struggles as a Child of God, I did things I promised I would never, ever do again. Yep, more dirt. As a nurse, I tend to be fascinated by what happens inside the body that makes its outward physical appearance change during a rampant infection. Mind you, most of my nursing experience comes from the geriatric population, but the physical body still operates the same.

Take, for example, a urinary tract infection. In an average person of good health, symptoms may be mild with some slight discomfort. It's easy to identify. One might go to the store and pick up some cranberry juice, drink plenty of extra fluids, maybe start taking some over-the-counter medications to ease the pain until you can flush your system out.

Ignore it, and the symptoms get worse. If you never had a severe one, good for you. God Bless. In the elderly folks, identifying it may not be so easy to diagnose. I have repeatedly seen personalities flip with the most out of character behaviors—combativeness, confusion, trouble concentrating, and lack of appetite. The list goes on. Left untreated, it could cause a severe blood infection and death. Here's another and one of my personal favorites. Again, it's the nurse in me—boils, abscesses, zits, and the like. What starts as a teeny-tiny break in the skin barrier has the potential to develop into something gnarly gross.

True story. I am known to watch videos of pimple popping purely for enjoyment. Just ask my kids. "Ew, mom! Why are you watching that?"

THINK ABOUT IT...

"Confess your sin and you shall be healed." Not my favorite verse currently in my walk. Admitting I had an addiction to pornography, self-loathing, depression, and suicidal ideations was hard for me confess out loud to my mentors. It was even harder to confess it to my pastors. I did not want to disappoint them. Obviously, I needed to go back to the basics.

There is not condemnation in Christ Jesus, and I am thankful for that. I can be honest and admit that is a truth I have not always walked in.

Remember there is nothing you have done that He hasn't already seen. And there is nothing that takes Him by surprise. My freedom and healing came from facing those demons head on and admitting some hard things. Once I did, I was restored.

The enemy will beat you up with condemnation if you let him.

It's the anticipation to see what comes out of something so obviously infected when pressure is applied, squeezed, or cut into. Some may ask the question: "How did it get so bad to have that much YUCK inside?"

It was there all along. For a long time. Waiting and building up until it started pushing its way to the surface and ready to explode. Such was the case with this dirty birdie. Royalty? Not so much. A royal mess? Absolutely. Not nearly as enjoyable to watch on replay.

But, for educational purposes, here is a list of

Father, I thank You that Your mercies are new every single day. As faithful as the sun comes up in the morning, so is the Blood of Jesus that washes and cleanses me from all unrighteousness. I confess out loud that I have failed you. Wash me and make me clean. By faith, I receive Your forgiveness. In Jesus name, so be it.

Lamentations 3:22-23

symptoms that should have sparked an opportunity for a Great Physician intervention that I chose to ignore: Fear, anxiety, depression, isolation, suicidal ideations, cursing, lack of prayer, lack of worship, lack of nutrition from the Word, engaging in activities I (believed to be) long past regressed. I settled on "just being." I told God more times than I could count: "Never mind. I don't want the present You have for me. I don't want it. No ministry. Nothing." (Of course, I lied.)

I was septic and parked in the wrong spot at the wrong hospital, and I invested in the wrong medical advice. Thankfully, this dirty bird was again rerouted, delivered from sin, demonic forces, and washed clean.

Weight Station – No More Twinkies

"Kathy, we are going to pick you up tomorrow, we are going to the mall, and you are going shopping. It is our gift to you," my sister demanded. "Ok, I relented."

It was Mother's Day Weekend. "It'll be nice to get out with my momma and sisters for a change," I thought. But I was still not sold on the idea of shopping for myself. It really has never been a hobby of mine. Sure, I'd buy the kids things, get nice decorative stuff for the house, and art supplies, but not clothes. Trying on any item of clothing was not an enjoyable experience. After all, I seemed to outgrow everything I owned up to this point. I was down to four sets of extra-large scrubs, a few T-shirts, and a single pair of jeans. Other than that, my wardrobe was nothing but pajamas. (Depressed much?)

The afternoon with my sisters and my mom was great. It had been several years since I actually had Mother's Day off, so I truly enjoyed my time with her. Fellowship was great. I didn't start to squirm until we went to a plus-sized women's store.

Growing up, I was super scrawny. I was a "string-bean" until I hit puberty. Then I became a "bubble butt." After each childbirth, I pretty well returned to my pre-pregnancy weight, roughly around one-fifty. After the birth of my third child, I fluctuated ten to twenty pounds. And initially, after the divorce, I was almost one-ninety, so I dieted and exercised to reach a more desired weight.

As I stood in the mirror, trying on my fourth pair of pants, I couldn't help but notice the damage I had done to my body. I was overweight, out of shape, out of breath, a field of belly rolls now contoured my natural femininity. I no longer had string-bean legs, and my bubble butt now had to hold up

THINK ABOUT IT...

Honoring my body as a temple of the Lord has not been my greatest strength.

When I started having physical symptoms of an ill-maintained temple, I had to really be honest with myself and take an honest inventory of how I was treating my body and why.

The how was much easier to correct than the why. The "why" is the root of what was going on inside. Shame, loneliness, fear, doubt, insecurity, isolation.

In every arena of my spiritual being there are roots. Some blossom into Great Pines, others into crabgrass.

Do you have weeds in your temple that causes your physical health to suffer?

two tires around my waist. My face looked like an over-inflated balloon that drooped under my chin. I did not feel pretty. I felt so embarrassed and ashamed. "Too many nights spent alone. Too many evenings off work with no one to fellowship with except a bag of Ruffles." I thought to myself. "No way am I doing

Father, I thank You for reminding me that my body is a temple. I ask that You reveal any needed adjustments I need to make so that I may continue to serve You, advance the Kingdom of Heaven, live a long and prosperous life that brings You glory. In Jesus name, so be it.

1 Corinthians 6:12-20

this to myself. I am not trying on any more clothes," I thought. I certainly didn't want my sisters to come into the stall to see how anything fit.

Though they were completely unaware of my inner dialogue, they continued with their mission until I let my guard down and found a nice "get-up" I felt good in.

After that, we went home. My baby sister cut and colored my hair and did my make-up. I felt like a million bucks. Granted, I still weighed the same. I didn't lose twenty pounds walking to the car.

I did, however, decide, "It's time to handle my body with my best interest in mind and invest in myself." I am worth it.

_____

_____

_____

_____

_____

_____

_____

_____

Falling Asleep at the Wheel - Closer

My room was dark—no noise except my box fan. I wasn't dreaming, and although I was rocked to sleep by the same obsession rolling around in my head by the night's ending, I was not prepared for the early morning visitor.

I had a plan. Finish the house repairs. Gather all my important financial information and put it in an open area for the boys to find. Write goodbye letters for my boys, my sisters, and my parents. Drive out to a secluded spot with my instrumentals near water to do the deed. I reviewed this plan nightly, making mental notations for corrections.

I must admit this ugly companion of mine had no real positive attributes except an offer for an easy out. I know just how selfish this was of me even to host such a cruel and selfish visitor. I am thankful I was allowed to see it, this spirit that desperately wanted to take me out. It completely caused me to rethink the current route in my journey.

I was coming out of a deep slumber (yeah, that's an excellent way to put it) when I had the feeling I was not alone in my room. Sometimes my kids walk through my room at night to use my bathroom, but this was not the case. I didn't hear the door open. The room was dark, but I felt a stranger's stare. I tapped my phone for a bit of light to shine, and there it was.

I know it sounds bizarre, but I saw it. A tall, dark shadow was standing right next to my bed. I felt his stare. I felt the intensity of its stare. I pulled the covers over my head and thought for a brief second how stupid it all would sound.

THINK ABOUT IT...

I somehow let the work of the cross and the blood of Jesus fall to the wayside. I let Satan have his way in my life for far too long. (Yes, I said that correctly.) I had the armor of God, but I chose to let it fall to the ground unused.

I believe right about now; the enemy knows he messed up big time. There is nothing greater than using the enemies own weapon against him. The spirit of suicide opens the door to depression, fear, anxiety, doubt, and pride.

Has there ever been in a battle when Holy Spirit tapped you on your shoulder to remind you to wear your armor?

Do you have someone you trust that you can confess to when you are tempted to give up or lay it all down?

Why is it important to reach out when we are tempted to give up?

Father, I thank You for the work of cross and the blood that poured out so that I can be healed, whole, and delivered. I thank You for the armor that the cross provided for me–and that is the blood of Jesus. I plead the blood of Jesus over my mind, my emotions, my past, my present and my future. In Jesus name, so be it.

Ephesians 1:7; 6:10-18
Revelation 12:11

Understand, I know the demonic realm is 100% real. But I've only heard stories from others who have experienced it. It didn't take long to feel that same stare intensifies and grow louder until I could hear it laughing at me. It was mocking me to do it. To go ahead and end my "pathetic life" because it didn't matter anyway.

Somehow, I was able to drift back into a light sleep. As I walked out of my house that morning for work, I looked around at the signs of life of my little family and caught a fresh reminder of everything God rescued me from. Assuredly, I went to work that day with an acute awareness that I have a real enemy who wants nothing more than to take me out. Suddenly, it didn't seem to be a viable option for me after all. I cried every time I thought about it and ended up reaching out to my dad after work to confess.

Shortly after, I found myself clinging to the cross and slowly drawing closer to Him once again.

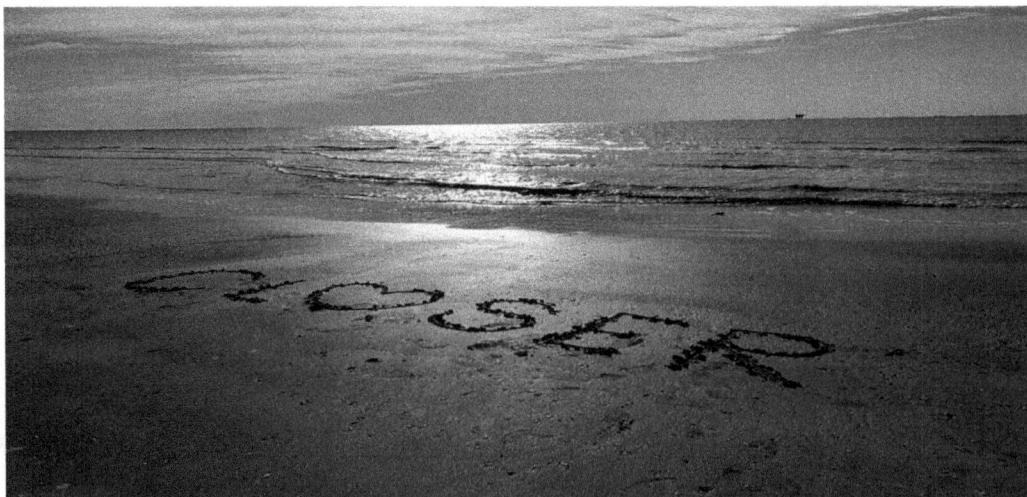

Getting Pulled-Over -The Weight of the Crown

I talked for over an hour to good friend of mine, Angelica, one night. We hadn't spoken in a while, though we had quick chats here and there. I read some of my short stories to her and showed her some of my artwork. As someone who also has a creative gift, I value her insight.

"You should write a story sometime about some of your drawings," she said to me. "You think?" I asked, admittedly not giving it much thought. I'd been working on the book and getting ready to finish it with much contemplation and prayer. The next morning, after sipping my first cup of coffee, I sunk back into my covers, thinking I could go back to sleep. I thought about Angelica advice and what these last final entries might look like.

For almost 20 years, I have been a follower of Jesus. I came to develop a personal relationship with Him during a challenging time in my life at the age of 28. Situations, circumstances, and even bigger than that, my own choices led me down a dark path of self-destruction until I had no other option except to look up. "Rescue" is the perfect word to describe my "come to Jesus" moment. I am so very thankful for the rescue that took place!

Walking with Jesus has been very fulfilling. I've learned so many things about myself, about Jesus, about the unrelenting love of God. I've crumbled time and again under the power of His love with the most beautiful indescribable revelations of Him, His Kingdom, His Word, of Holy Spirit by Holy Spirit.

I've soaked in His presence and oozed it out over a hurting and dying world. I tasted only a nibble of my assignment on this earth, and it indeed is delicious. I've been full-on the

THINK ABOUT IT...

I thought I knew everything I needed to know about who I was at one time. Silly me. Before, I veered off into the desert, I was on our prayer team.

I made inner vows I would never go back to the wretched and wicked ways I came from. Compromise is something most of us are familiar with.

I certainly did not understand everything I was feeling during this season and why I was feeling it. I had every tool at my disposal to break free.

Admittedly, I chose not to. At least until that familiar wooing came knocking on the door of my heart again.

No lie from the enemy can keep me from answering that knock. I wanted everything I knew God promised me. Let that be your prayer today.

goodness of God. I could write forever on the things He has done for me.

And yet, parts of it have become a terrifying journey as well. I know, I know, this sounds crazy, yet contradictory. Let me assure you, friends, the "terror" I speak of, has been a product of my own decisions and not from storms or attacks of the enemy.

Writing this section, and exposing it, is like dragging out the mistress in my closet by her hair to expose her to the world–her name is Compromise. Everybody knows her. She is a stranger to no one.

Compromise and I became pretty close over the last four years. We have had quick exchanges here and there, but I turned to Compromise for comfort when fear came. I would pray, worship, journal, and go to church and suddenly be aware that I was carrying the stench of her visit. I ran to the altar to shower and be made clean. Soon after, I would invite her back over and, as it goes, Compromise made herself at home. In developing our affair, we engaged in bitterness, unforgiveness, sexual sin, selfishness, addiction, and depression.

And she was so kind to bring me a blanket of shame.

Shame kept me shackled to Compromise. Shame paved the way for isolation from my friends and church family.

"You know better, Katherine."

"You know the Word of God."

"Now, God can't use you. You missed it—big time. You ruined any chance of ever being in ministry. Your anointing is gone. You probably weren't even called in the first place. Look at what a mess you made. It's over. It's over for you, for your kids, for your future. You aren't going anywhere."

I can still hear these lies. Yes, lies. I recognized them then as lies but continued the cycle until I finally became desperate enough to break free. I had yet another choice to make. (I am so, so, so thankful for the hound-dog of Holy Spirit that chases us down!)

This morning as I reflected on where I was spiritually at the time, Holy Spirit dropped this picture into my mind:

Soft worship played as I sketched this. Tears fell during every phase of creating this piece.

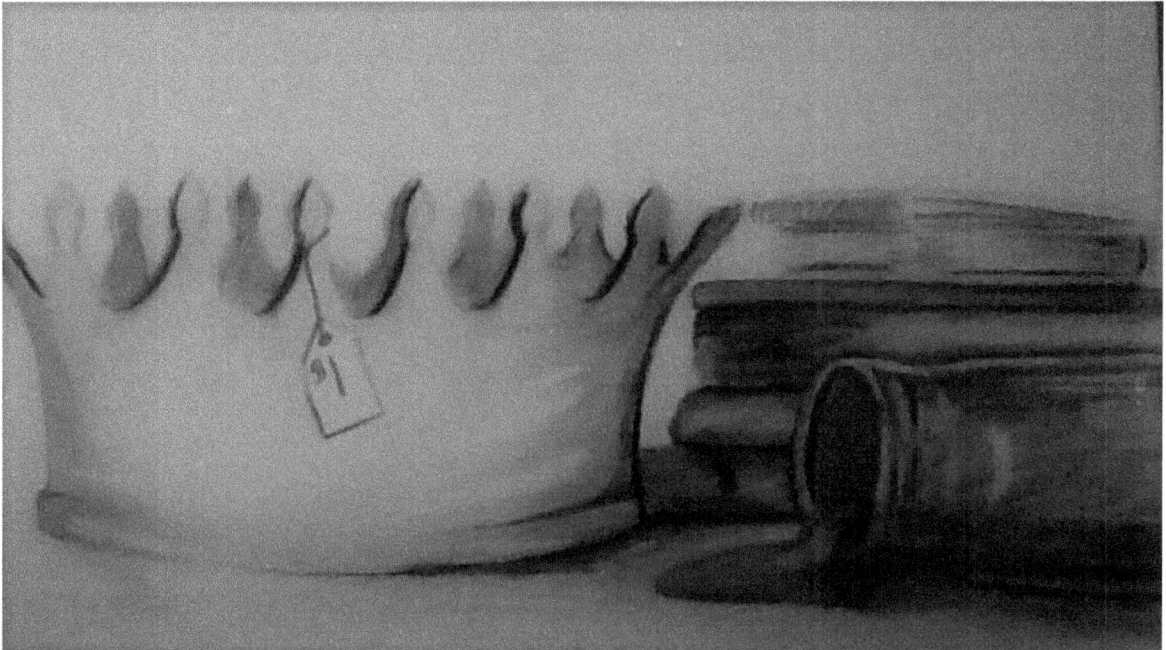

I journaled in prayer:

"Oh, the weight of the crown. Father, I treated the precious gift You gave me as a plastic child's play toy. I tossed it onto the table along with every good thing You gave to me. I am broken in grief right now. The image You gave me of my crown, my bible, my journals, my armor, and the anointing laid out on a table at a cheap garage sale. The weight of the crown and all it stands for laid out as unwanted, unvalued, and undesirable junk.

I am so sorry. I am so sorry, Father. The sale is over! The sale is over! You repurchased it at a high price indeed. My Father, My King, put my crown back on my head. Help me to feel the weight of my crown once again."

_____

_____

_____

_____

Father, I thank You for Your relentless pursuit of me. Forgive me of all compromise and for tossing my crown to the wayside. I understand I was bought with the blood of Jesus-a high price. Help me to walk in my new identity in You and live out the promises You have given me. Help me to feel the weight of the crown and understand the mandate that comes with it. In Jesus name, so be it.

Isaiah 62:3

Checking the Map – Connecting the Dots

Sometimes wandering out in the desert can be likened to getting lost on the "loop." When I am driving into unfamiliar territory and seeing landmarks, I know I've already been there, and I'm still going the wrong way. Other times, I might see something that I missed the first time, which causes an abrupt turnaround, or I start to see a pattern of familiarity. Either way, the end of my isolation/desert wandering period was ending abruptly.

While I could not put a pin in my direct location, I was still taking in the sights. I started doing a lot of artwork. Not for any specific reason except maybe to just keep my mind occupied. Mind you; I cannot lie to anyone (much less myself or God) and say that I was where I needed or wanted to be on my journey. But I can say with all integrity-towards the end; I wanted to be where He wanted me. I know it sounds crazy.

I painted several pictures. I bought all kinds of supplies: paint, brushes, canvases of all types and sizes. I painted several lovely pieces and shared them with friends and family. Then I bought up charcoal and pencil supplies. I was excited I could still draw in pencil with even more detail than when I was a teen. I would have an idea pop into my head, and in no time-there it was. I would sketch it out and stand back in awe of how good it looked. A key. A showerhead with running water. Blue jeans. A nurse running. Raindrops. An umbrella. My dog. My old room at our old trailer. Me as a child.

Intermittently, I would get a nudge to type out some of my experiences with God. "Stories" that I am deeply attached to. Stories that I often tell that brings the excitement of my first love up to the surface. I figured, if nothing else, they were for Him and me. Maybe my children would love to

THINK ABOUT IT...

Finally, here is the fun part. This was my favorite part of putting this whole book together.

Connecting the dots, solving the puzzle, putting who He created me to be to see the bigger picture. My crown. My mandate. Now it is your turn. Take every piece— the good, the bad, the ugly. Take every minute detail you can "see" the thumbprint of Jesus on.

What do you see?

Do you see how He kept you? Healed you? Protected and guided you? Saved you from yourself? Saved you from the grips of bondage? A king does not pardon and bless just anyone. He does not keep the door to His private chambers open for all access to just anyone. He does for His own though. You are His.

A Royal Priesthood, a chosen people. You are Royalty.

have them to read to their children when I am gone. But right in the middle of the fourth "story," a light went off, and there was that familiar voice I thought I long forgot.

"This is your book. This is Road to Royalty."

I sat there for a moment in silence, pondering this. What? No way.

"Katherine, this is YOUR Road to Royalty. Your road is uniquely yours. Tell your story." Almost immediately, I started having all sorts of creative ideas of how to put this together. I won't bore you'll with my ideas, though. I continued to write as Holy Spirit brought to remembrance each event. Story after story. Everything was in place the way "I thought it should be laid out. I would think, "Maybe I need to do an illustration," then Holy Spirit would remind me, "Nope, you already did one." Sure enough, I would go looking for it, and there it was. I almost edited some of the sketches but was sharply directed not to.

My dad told me one afternoon while I was talking to him about it, "Sugar, you might ought to think about putting it together in chronological order. That way, everyone can understand you and where you are coming from. It makes it more real."

"Well, who is he to give me advice with my super anointed creative mind to tell me what to do with my book?!" Shame on me, but this was what I thought about my dad's input. Out of sight, out of mind. Or so I thought until I started getting to where I am right now.

I took Dad's advice and put them in order. I wrote every headline on a sticky pad and laid them out. As I was organizing, I felt my destiny snap back into place as each piece began to fit perfectly together, and I could see it all being unfolded right before my eyes. (Enter snot and tears here.)

I saw how the enemy tried desperately to hide my identity from me, even after being born again. I saw how years of rejection kept me from truly believing that I was worthy of ever being a daughter of the King, much less worthy of being in ministry. I saw all the underlying events that took place-many of which I did not even write about-that occurred that caused me to wear such deceptive lenses. Even though I thought I knew it all, the weight of the Kingdom hit my spirit as I stared down at my map, and it all came together. Every experience and every prophetic word mingled and fused together with what I knew He called me to do- instantly snapped back into place. My eyes are open. I knew before I was a child of Abba God. Now, I KNOW I am a daughter of the KING.

AND I AM ...

Royalty.

_____

_____

_____

_____

Father, thank You for helping me to feel the crown You have placed upon my head. Thank You for opening my eyes to every fingerprint and mark of approval. I ask that as I go forward, I have Your eyes to see, Your heart to love, Your words in my mouth as I carry out the orders I have received from the King of Kings. I understand I have not just been made Royalty for the title, but for the mandate. In Jesus name, so be it.

1 Peter 2:9

_____

_____

_____

_____

_____

Welcome Home

Upon completion of **Road to Royalty**, I chose visual imagery to relay the primary purpose of this book. Hence, the book cover. We see a beautiful woman in her bridal attire, with her crown walking along a dirt road headed straight into a beautiful sunrise. Off to the side behind her is a pair of old worn-out discarded tennis shoes.

I am that woman. I purposefully removed those old shoes (that represent a striving, begging, less than mentality) and donned my royal attire. I purposefully position myself to walk toward the Son in my new identity. So, what does it mean to be "Royalty" any way?

On this side of healing and deliverance, we can now have a new sense of freedom and discovery. We are no longer that child hiding in the dark begging to found. We are no longer paupers begging for acceptance and affections from the heart. Because, once we have made Jesus our Lord and Savior, we have been adopted into the Kingdom of God. We are joint Heirs and destined to reign with Christ the King.

A Prayer for Salvation

A Prayer to Accept Jesus as Savior

Dear Heavenly Father,
I believe that Jesus died for me.
I believe that Jesus paid for my sins on the cross.
I believe that Jesus rose from the dead.
I ask you to forgive me of my sins. I ask you to wash me clean of all sin.
I put my faith and trust in Jesus as my only hope for living eternally with you in heaven.

I ask Jesus to be my Savior and my Lord. I want to live my life for Christ.
I understand that my salvation is not based on my works but on the sacrifice of
Jesus on the cross.
Thank you for saving me!
Amen!

Artistic

Expressions

(Prophetic Poetry & Art By Katherine)

Think About it...

It's just like when you were little

Small feet in Daddy's shoes

Working to make each piece fit

To make every rough edge smooth

If I'd told you how I'd do it

There's no way you would believe

Step back into the mirror

Child, you're ROYALTY.

Think About it...

Think about every single moment

Think about all that you've been through

Think about every time you heard Me say

"Child, I'm still with You."

Think about every single mountain

And every valley low

There's no place that you have been

That I left you alone

Think about it...

Think about every single moment

Every storm you couldn't see

Think about every single struggle

When you called to Me

Think about each and every hard time

That I covered you in peace

Think about the crown your wearing

Child, you're ROYALTY.

Think about it...

Don't forget your triumphs

And all the good we've done

In case you have forgot it all.

Child, we've just begun.

You're ROYALTY.

Think about it...

I put a ring upon your finger.

And a crown upon your head.

Wrapped a rope around your shoulders

I Am the Great I Am

You're ROYALTY

Think about it...

Walk With Me

One morning while reading the Bible and journaling, this image came to mind along with a deep personal revelation of what it looks like when I am seeking Him in my day to day...

Treasure

Like an old child's plaything

That's lost all her appeal.

She was tossed out on a trash heap...

And crushed under her will.

She's buried amongst the garbage.

Covered in mud and broken up.

All she wanted was a purpose.

All she wanted was to be loved.

Now the sun is out, and the storm has passed.

Her hair is matted down-

Where is the smile that lit the room?

Where is her bridal gown?

I picked her up

Out of the trash heap.

I made her clean.

I washed her hair.

I gave her a new name.

And a brand-new gown to wear.

There's no scars.

There's no patches.

There are no wounds left to heal.

Her smile is brighter now than ever...

She's been restored

For My will.

There's nothing else that brings Me more pleasure-

Than to make someone else's trash My treasure.

Back Roads

I'll take the back roads any day
Enjoy the scenery on the way

Cruise real slow just to take in
everything
I'll take the back roads.

I'll take the back roads every time
Turn off chatter in my mind
Sometimes I just need to turn around.
And take the back roads.

I'm not cutting any corners.
I'm not breaking any rules.
Real change only happens
when I choose to follow You...

Color Me Beautiful

You formed me in secret
With a purpose and design
Every color marks Your talent.
Your beauty is mine.
On a canvas of Your nature
As A treasure on display
I am beautifully adorned.

In Your gallery of grace.

"My creation of you did not stop in your mother's womb. I continue to paint even in your pain and hard seasons. Even in your "secret" pain. Remember that all things work together-every color-of triumphs and struggles...bright colors and dark colors on every spectrum. I use them all. And yes-you are a trophy of Grace."

You Were There

Before I was born,
You were there.
My first words and nimble steps,
You were there.
When I wore my heart on my sleeve,
You were there.
When jealousy was born,
You were there.
When I tried and failed to fit in,
You were there.
When I tried over and over again to know You,
You were there.
Lessons unlearned,
You were there.
When my sister left,
You were there.
When I needed a friend,
You were there.
Rinse and repeat, rinse, and repeat,
You were there.
When I turned on You,
You were there.
When I lied to myself,
You were there.
When I tried by myself to make myself happy,
You were there.
When I had my babies,
You were there.
When my world fell apart,
You were there.
When I needed You,
You were there.
When I needed healing,
You were there.
When I was destitute,
You were there.
When I had no job,
You were there.

When I needed love,
You were there.
When I was lonely,
You were there.
When I was hungry,
 You were there.
When I was full,
 You were there.
When I had love,
You were there.
When I questioned,
You were there.
When I turned away from You,
You were there.
When I was mad at You,
You were there.
When I ran,
You were there.
When I made excuses,
You were there.
When I chose pain,
You were there.
When I felt You calling,
You were there.
When I came running,
You were there.

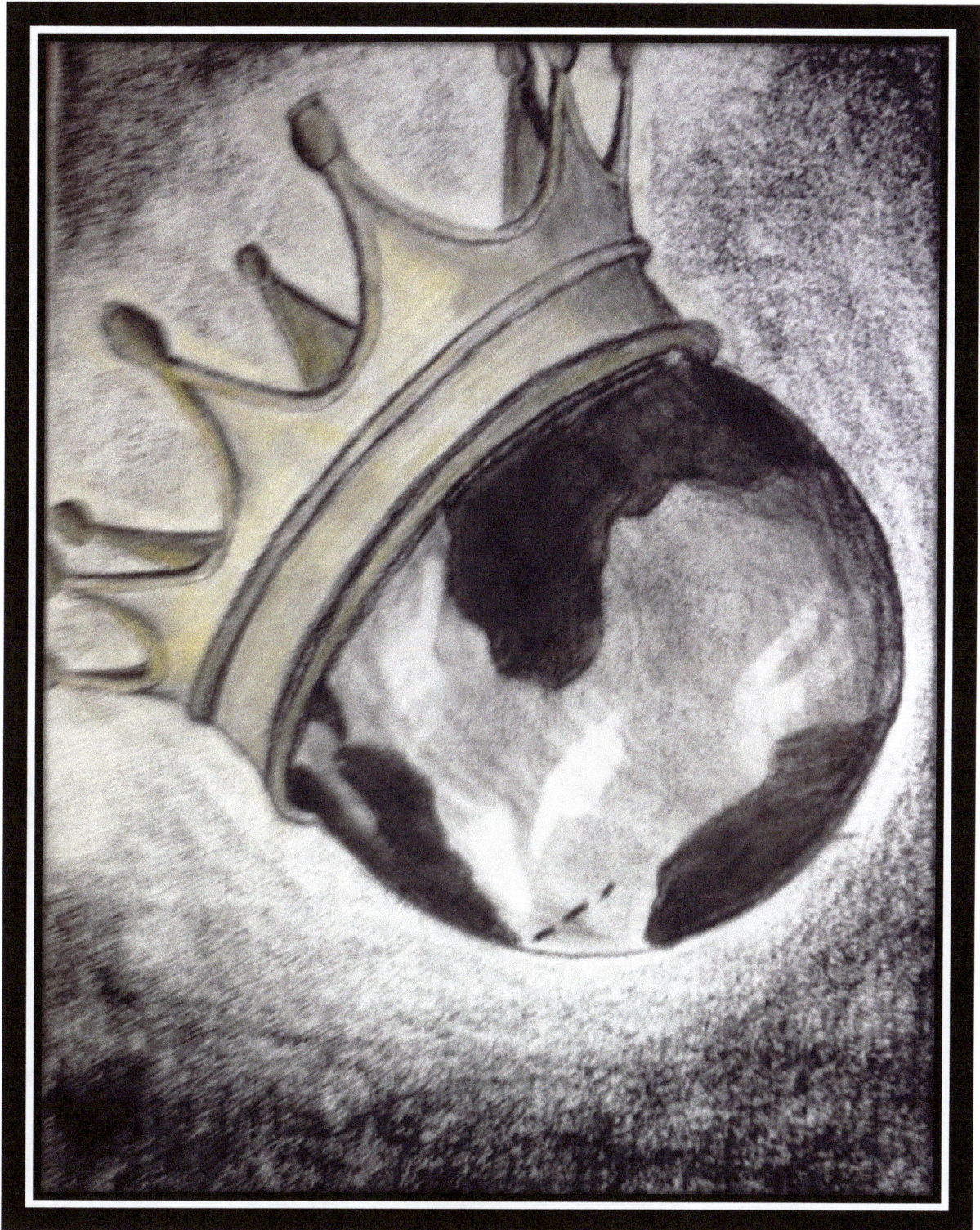

Closer ...

Than a brother.

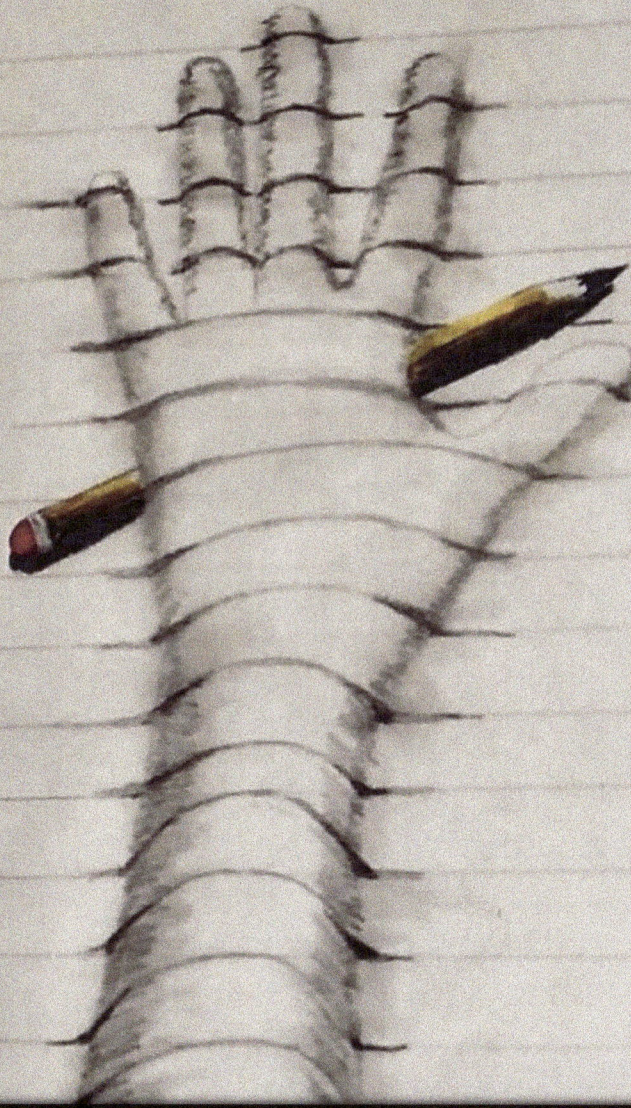

It may be my story, but I'm not the Author.

Author Bio

Katherine Renteria, born in Baytown, Texas, grew into a young, family-oriented woman with a passion for serving and helping others who could not help themselves. She is a geriatric nurse as well as a passionate lover of Jesus of Christ. She developed many natural gifts over the years, including writing poetry, short stories, songs, painting, and sketching. In the spiritual realm, she flows dynamically in teaching, prophetic and healing gifts. She has a passion for women's broken hearts to see them healed, restored to their God-given identity and purpose while living in the fullness of SOZO life.

Contact Information

Email: roadtoroyalty@gmail.com

Website: www.krenteria.com

Facebook: @ksrenteria